THE COMPLETE

Conference Organiser's

HANDBOOK

ROBIN O'CONNOR

PIATKUS

First published in 1994 by
Judy Piatkus (Publishers) Ltd
5 Windmill Street, London W1P 1HF

First paperback edition 1994

*A catalogue record for this book is
available from the British Library*

ISBN 0–7499–1176–X hbk
　　　0–7499–1408–4 pbk

Edited by Carol Franklin
Designed by Paul Saunders

*IBM is a Registered Trade Mark of
International Business Machines, Inc.
Kodak and Carousel are Registered Trade
Marks of Kodak Ltd.*

Set in Linotron Times by
Phoenix Photosetting, Chatham
Printed and bound in Great Britain by
Biddles Ltd, Guildford and King's Lynn

CONTENTS

INTRODUCTION

This is a book about conferences – but first we need a definition of a conference to start us off. A simple dictionary definition is '. . . a meeting for consultation, exchange of information, or discussion', but practised conference organisers, producers and delegates have long been aware that conferences can offer much more than that.

When it is well-planned and executed, a conference can enthuse a salesforce; it can create a new image for a company among its shareholders and staff; successfully launch an unfamiliar new product to a trade audience; persuade employees to change working methods or techniques; and more than almost any other corporate communication medium it can let people speak to each other more effectively, helping them celebrate success more triumphantly or analyse failure more perceptively.

A conference does not have to be gigantic or expensive to be important. Two executives meeting to agree a change in strategy can be as critical to a company's success as a well-orchestrated, 1,000-strong sales convention. Both events have objectives; recognising those objectives and creating the environment in which they may be achieved effectively and economically is the conference organiser's job.

Few companies can afford the luxury of a full-time conference organiser on their staff, so it is likely that the task will fall to a staff member who already has enough to do performing his or her own regular company duties. If you are that person, then this book is addressed to you – and whether you decide to go outside the company for specialist help to stage the event or to use in-house resources to supply the skills you need, I hope that the following pages will give you a great deal of practical help and information.

THE MEDIUM

Among all the forms of corporate communication, the conference medium is almost certainly the most exciting, frustrating, rewarding and memorable. It is 'live', just like the theatre, and in some forms of conference presentation borrowing show-business techniques to present business matters can make a great deal of sense. In the theatre writers, directors, actors and designers join forces not only to entertain audiences, but also at times to move them, to inform them, even to change their opinions. In business too, it is often necessary to change the way people think, to present unfamiliar information or to heighten the emotional temperature of an audience, so it often makes good sense to enlist many of the techniques used in the professional theatre. Perhaps the reason it isn't done more often is cost – a word that is uppermost in the minds of all conference organisers, whatever type of event they are planning.

CUTTING THE COST

Mounting a company conference which aims to impart its messages effectively and professionally has become an increasingly expensive matter. A well-planned and executed event demands a great deal of thought, at least some specialised skills and a particular kind of creativity not usually demanded of company staff. Reducing the size of the conference by carefully pruning the number of delegates and selecting a smaller, less expensive venue has obvious cost advantages; but if the event is to be effective and memorable – in fact, worth doing at all – it will still be necessary for someone to plan it carefully, to create it imaginatively and to produce it effectively.

Is it possible for a company to 'go it alone', to produce its own conference, using as many 'in-house' skills as possible, buying in the talents and equipment it needs to mount an effective presentation? In my view, and depending very much on the size and nature of the event, the answer is a qualified 'yes'. There are advantages in 'doing it yourself' of course, one being that no one knows your business like you do so there'll be no risk of an 'outsider' misunderstanding the way you operate. Also, many companies develop their own internal 'language' over the years – words and phrases which have a special meaning within the company – so surely the best person to use this 'language' most knowledgeably and effectively would be you or a member of your own staff. And then there is the compelling argument that 'doing it yourself' saves the often considerable cost of using a professional production house.

There are pitfalls, however. How do you go about creating a conference that will work? Can you find the skills within your company to write it, produce it, direct it? If you do find staff with these skills, can you afford to pay for them in terms of hours lost on 'normal' work? And where do you go to find the skills and facilities you don't have in-house – the venue-booking expertise, the technical equipment you may need and so on?

Perhaps you decide to turn to a professional conference production house to take your brief and turn it into an exciting, memorable event. Employing such a specialised resource is unlikely to be cheap, but if you consider your conference important you'll be measuring cost-effectiveness rather than cost alone. The production house staff will have the best incentive of all for delivering the goods – they want to be asked to produce your next conference – so there's every likelihood you'll get what you're paying for. But how do you select the right production company? And how can you get maximum value from them by playing an active and knowledgeable role in the production process?

For example, if the production house team didn't get all the necessary information, or it wasn't detailed enough, there's almost certain to be a cost penalty waiting to be paid somewhere down the line. Did the production house personnel really understand your business? Yes, it's their job to do just that, and although the vast majority succeed in a way that's little short of uncanny, some businesses have internal subtleties that defy interpretation by even their longest-serving employees. And again, although you may know the precise cost of goods and services you buy-in regularly, how can you be sure you are getting maximum value from the often sizeable sums you are spending on your relatively infrequent conferences?

For the past eighteen years I've been providing answers to

those questions for some of the leading companies in the UK and abroad. After working as an advertising copywriter, and as a writer and producer in television, in 1974 I turned to the corporate market at a time when the value of effective communication was beginning to be recognised. Since then I've written and directed a vast number of conferences, programmes and presentations for some of the country's leading companies, in the process gathering a great deal of experience – and making quite a few mistakes – which in these pages I hope to turn into practical information aimed at helping you make your conference less costly and more effective.

Whether you choose a professional production house to handle your event or decide to produce some or all of its elements in-house, *The Complete Conference Organiser's Handbook* will, among many other topics:

• show you how to plan and produce an event using your own in-house resources;

• help you select a short-list of the most appropriate production houses and venues;

• show you how to produce a concise, clear brief minimising the possibility of misunderstanding – and extra costs – at a later stage;

• present a detailed conference check-list enabling you to plan and monitor the progress of your event;

• describe how various conference events are created, written and produced, and how in-house resources may effectively be used to carry out these operations;

• provide a clear, non-technical guide to the function and use of technical equipment commonly used in the conference field;

• review the latest conference techniques – such as teleconferencing; and

• demonstrate a simple method of measuring the effectiveness of your conference.

Added to all this information is one more feature which I believe makes this book unique. Linked to each chapter and subject is a services guide, a directory of companies and individuals offering a wide range of services and skills of particular relevance to corporate conference organisers. This guide, together with the practical information contained in the rest of the book, should enable corporate personnel at all levels to gain a better understanding of the potential of this powerful communication tool.

The aim has been to provide you with a practical, working knowledge of conference technicalities and techniques. Armed with that knowledge, you will control the medium more efficiently – and make it work for you even more effectively.

Masculine terms are used frequently throughout the text; I hope this doesn't offend the high proportion of women associated with the conference business but I wanted to avoid the visually irritating s/he or tiresome repetition of 'him or her'. My apologies to all female producers and clients, without whom the conference world would probably cease to exist.

Robin O'Connor

1 WHAT MAKES A CONFERENCE?

- The sales conference ● The press conference
- The corporate presentation ● The financial presentation
- The annual general meeting ● The road show
- The product launch ● Special event productions
- Exhibitions ● Seminars and symposia ● Training
- Teleconferencing

For the purposes of this book a conference is defined as any gathering of people who meet to achieve an objective. It's a pretty loose definition, but conferences are difficult things to pin down; they're all different, the objectives they set out to achieve vary greatly and it's possible to use a wide variety of techniques to hit the conference target.

What is that target? The answer is that it is simply to convey what is in your mind to the audience – a thought that's well worth remembering when you sit down to plan a conference. It's also worth remembering that you start with one major advantage over many other forms of corporate communication; you'll probably have a very good idea of the nature of your audience – indeed, you may know some, if not all, of the delegates personally.

In later chapters we'll be taking a detailed look at planning and producing a conference, but let's start by examining a number of different conference categories, at their probable aims, at the types of audiences likely to attend and at some of the techniques used to produce these events. A word of warning first: attempting to subject 'the conference' to any form of rigid classification is doomed to failure. Your event will most probably contain elements from more than one of the following categories with other features added to suit your particular needs and those of your audience.

THE SALES CONFERENCE

There is no 'typical' sales conference. The size may range from half a dozen people gathered together in a hotel conference suite to hundreds packed into a giant exhibition hall. Styles vary too; the smaller events are often quiet and businesslike with the subdued clack of computer keys calling up information screens the only reminder that technology has a part to play in the presentation process; while at the other extreme some larger sales conferences have been conducted with all the raging fervour of a Revivalist prayer meeting, aided by technology which wouldn't disgrace a heavy metal pop group!

The style of the sales conference should be dictated by its aim. And the aim of any conference is to communicate with an audience.

Audiences

Salespeople can be the toughest audiences in the world. They're at the sharp end of your business and they know better than anyone the true worth of your products. If you want to launch a new widget that's still in development and the flange keeps falling off don't announce the new product's arrival with a flourish of trumpets at your sales conference. If the people in your salesforce are any good they'll find out about that wayward flange soon enough and bang goes your credibility next time around. Never underestimate salespeople. It's arrogant, it's insulting and – if you've hired the right people – it's unnecessary.

A salesforce audience can be tough in another way too. Any given salesforce will most likely consist of a bewildering variety of people – some will be young, some older, there'll be men and women, serious types, eccentrics, pop music fans, opera buffs, all sorts. You couldn't imagine all these people individually choosing to go to one, single event – so why should they all enjoy and profit from your sales conference? The answer is that they won't – unless you plan the event around some unifying factor.

Techniques

What presentational techniques do you need to consider when preparing a sales conference? Is your primary need to inform your audience of a tactical change to your sales plans or to bring them up to date with complex developments in your market? If so, a fairly low-key approach is indicated, using technology sparingly and only to support what your speakers have to say.

Or do you want to send a group of salespeople out into the market bristling with enthusiasm, ravenously eager to achieve the sales targets you've set? In that case your sales conference should act as a dynamo, generating a sense of energy and purpose with enough momentum to motivate its audience throughout the year. What is indicated here is an Event with a capital E, something that is entertaining, exciting and above all memorable, so this type of sales conference might borrow theatrical elements – such as lavish sets, big-name presenters and some of the latest presentation technology.

Between these two extremes lies a wide range of sales conference styles – and the style you choose should be determined by the objectives you set for the event and by the nature of the audience. This seems too obvious to need stating, but it is surprising how many companies embark on productions which are either so spectacular it's difficult to discern the serious message behind them; or so starkly minimalist as to strangle at birth any enthusiasm the audience might have felt as the curtain went up.

Your salespeople are vital to the success of your business, and the sales conference offers a wonderful opportunity to meet and talk to them all. It's also perhaps the best opportunity you'll have to transmit to them your company's image of success and – equally important – to hear their reactions, so it is essential to plan and execute the event with imagination, with insight and with great care.

THE PRESS CONFERENCE

The audience

Journalists are hard-bitten, not easily impressed, write what they want to, not what you tell them and have an unerring instinct for locating the nearest bar. That may be true of some members of the profession, but on the whole it is better to think of the journalists who attend your press conferences as well-informed professionals with particularly enquiring minds, who are eager to fill space with genuinely newsworthy copy and who will faithfully transmit your message if you've taken the trouble to present it in a clear, concise fashion.

Avoid 'talking down' to your audience, but aim for simplicity; the majority of journalists attending your press conference will probably have a very good understanding of your business and its market, so laboriously spelling out your message won't go down too well with them. But there will be some who are on unfamiliar ground and you should remember them as you prepare your presentation; they'll thank you for your clarity, while their more experienced colleagues can easily take the opportunity to seek out more details at question time.

Techniques

Presenting information clearly is the key requirement of a press conference. Speakers should be accustomed to addressing such audiences – and should be trained to do so if they are not; spoken material ought to be prepared and rehearsed well before the event if possible; questions from the floor should be anticipated and these too should be rehearsed with colleagues acting the roles of 'hostile' journalists; and consideration should be given to supporting the main speaker at the event with colleagues able to field specialist questions.

The information displayed on any visual support material for speakers should be clear. Slides should contain no more than twenty words or thirty figures. If a concept is too complex to portray visually with any degree of precision, don't risk misleading your audience by oversimplification. If it needs elaboration, elaborate – either by producing a series of visuals that reveal the concept step by step or by explaining the matter clearly in a carefully prepared speech.

A press conference is not the place to flex technological muscles. If you do decide to use some form of visual support, keep the technology simple. A single slide projector, a series of caption boards or a previously prepared flip chart could be all you'll need. Your audience is expecting to hear news and that's best delivered by a real, live, human being.

If you have video or film material that's relevant to your message, use it by all means, but only after double-checking the equipment on the spot, rehearsing with the technicians who will operate it – and making absolutely sure everyone in the audience can see the material comfortably. Forcing journalists to peer at a small, dim screen where pictures don't appear on cue won't do a great deal for your company image. Make sure you have some control over room lighting and, if you are expecting a large audience, consider using a number of small video screens instead of a single, large one.

Whatever your press conference message, it should be repeated clearly in the press pack given to journalists before they leave. And do make sure it's repeated accurately; printed facts or details should tally precisely with what's been said at the conference, a point that's occasionally overlooked with embarrassing consequences. The long lead-times of conventional printing processes were often to blame for press packs containing wrong information, but with the rise of desk-top publishing and its ability to produce attractive print very quickly, this should no longer be a problem.

THE CORPORATE PRESENTATION

Although corporate presentations are produced in many forms, a common aim is usually to inform a target audience of the qualities of a company, its operation or its products. The presentation methods and techniques used can vary greatly depending upon the composition of the audience and the presentation location.

Audiences

The audience may consist of company staff, for example, in which case the presentation would probably be held on company premises and might include live speakers with visual support provided by slides or video. In this type of presentation the intention is often to explain a change in corporate structure, the introduction of new working methods or some other internal matter.

Computer presentation techniques

The use of the computer in producing corporate presentations held in-house is a growing trend. Capable of producing colourful, easily understood graphic images quickly and at far less cost than conventional artwork, the computer also has the capability to act as a presentation medium in its own right and has been seen as a perfect way to produce presentations which need to be made frequently and often at short notice. In a perfect computer world (still to come despite – or maybe because of – the enthusiasm of computer salespeople), it should be possible to use the office computer network to play out your presentation to selected staff members in their own working locations – there will be no need for them to gather together in a separate room to see and hear what you have to say.

Using this technique has undoubted advantages if the content of the presentation is predominantly informative – updating staff on the current state of the market for example – but it's perhaps less suitable as a medium for transmitting enthusiasm, for motivating. If your corporate presentation is asking staff for co-operation, for understanding or for effort then exposing them to disembodied messages on a VDU screen is perhaps not the best way to get it! A networked computer presentation may look slick and impressive, but ask yourself – or better still, ask your staff – if it's getting your message across effectively. If that message involves some inspirational element, you'll almost certainly find you'll get far better results by meeting people face to face. It may be harder work for you – computer presentations don't normally invite personal interaction – but by speaking to your staff directly they will feel more involved and you'll get immediate feedback – invaluable when you're trying to assess how well your message has been received.

Video and slide/tape presentations

Corporate presentations are also often made to potential buyers, clients or the general public – on exhibition stands for example, or in connection with a business or trade event. These sometimes take the form of self-contained video programmes or slide/tape presentations promoting a company and/or its product so they perhaps fall outside our conference definition. In common with other events, however, they have to be planned, written and produced so the information given later on in this book remains relevant.

THE FINANCIAL PRESENTATION

Audiences

Broadly speaking, audiences for financial presentations fall into two groups: those who understand financial matters and those who don't. In general, audiences for financial presentations tend to be fairly small – no more than twenty to thirty perhaps – but some financial element is often included as part of a larger event – such as an AGM for example – where many more people from both groups will be present.

Techniques

For smaller, specialist audiences visual aids are used mainly to reinforce a message or to illustrate broad concepts. Intricate financial detail is not easily conveyed on slides or OHP (overhead projector) transparencies; and video material, although allowing animation which helps to clarify complex processes, can be expensive to produce and would probably be inappropriate for a fairly intimate gathering. Computer-prepared material displayed on a VDU, a number of screens or on a projection system could both illustrate detail and simplify complexity, but there's a danger here. A slick, impressive 'state-of-the-art' computer presentation may fill your audience with wonder, but unless it's very carefully planned it might not fill them with equal amounts of comprehension. As ever, the paramount need is to communicate your message to the audience and the computer provides just one way of doing that, not necessarily the best.

Preparing a presentation for an audience with little or no knowledge of the financial world requires a great deal of thought – and possibly the services of a writer or producer with as little knowledge of finance as the audience. In my view, creating a financial presentation which makes sense to the layperson is not a job for a financial expert. In fact, any presentation of a specialist subject to a non-specialist audience is best created by someone whose only specialisation is communication. To see what happens when you let specialists loose on their own pet subject, turn to virtually any early form of computer documentation. Things only began to change for the better in the computer world after a huge computer manufacturer discovered that the documentation secretly being used by its own staff wasn't the 'official' version, but a simple instruction sheet written by a secretary, who knew nothing about computers, but understood how to operate one and how to pass that information on to others equally ignorant of the computer's mysteries.

Visual aids

For most financial presentations to general audiences, visual aids are essential. Many financial activities involve movement – of money, of properties or of companies, for example – and these movements or changes will be more easily understood by a lay audience through graphic images, particularly if those images can be animated. A twin-projector slide presentation unit allows images to be cut or dissolved from one to another, giving a fair representation of movement, but perhaps the most effective medium here is video. The range of visual effects now possible on video is almost limitless, making it invaluable for illustrating even the most rarefied financial activity. To take just one example, imagine trying to explain financial gearing to a layperson without being able to show how the ratio of a company's debt to its equity capital changes from time to time.

As with the press conference, it's wise to produce the salient features of your financial presentation in printed form for distribution to your audience either before or after the event. Whether you are presenting to financial specialists or laypersons it's also a very good idea to prepare answers to every conceivable question – or to have people with you who know what those answers might be. And – unless there's a very good reason for it – avoid comedy, particularly if you are seeking your audience's approval of expenditure or their own investment. Money is serious. But it needn't be dull.

THE ANNUAL GENERAL MEETING

Audiences

Planning and executing an AGM for a large company with many shareholders can be a mammoth task. How many shareholders are likely to attend the event? Just because 1,000 turned up last year don't automatically assume the numbers will remain the same; changes to your share price or your market sector might awaken interest in many shareholders who wouldn't normally go near an AGM and you could find an embarrassingly large number turning up. A reply-paid invitation to attend the AGM sent with the statement and accounts well in advance of the event should produce enough response to give some indication of whether you should book the Albert Hall or a room in a local hotel.

A shareholder audience can comprise a bewildering diversity of people – everyone from the small investor with little or no knowledge of your company and its operation to the dangerously well-informed professional investor who not only knows exactly what you are doing and why, but also what your competitors are up to. Satisfying both these groups in an event which must run more or less to time is difficult, but with adequate preparation and a realistic appreciation of the mood of the audience it's not impossible.

You may not be able to anticipate every question from the floor, but if the event as a whole is generating the desired 'atmosphere' of approval among shareholders, any rogue questions designed to cast doubt upon the proceedings may be isolated and dealt with far more easily.

Platform personalities

Most AGMs are as much to do with personalities as they are with financial performance. From the shareholders' point of view the people who speak from the platform are the guardians of their funds, so although the officers of the company should by all means exhibit a certain amount of entrepreneurial energy their words, actions and general demeanour should perhaps tend towards prudence, wisdom and foresight. This can be a matter of presentation; a shirt-sleeved, fast-talking *Wunderkind* may be undeniably exciting, but if it were *your* money wouldn't you rather it were in the hands of someone who spoke in slow, measured phrases and wore a dark suit?

Techniques

Similarly, it's rarely a good idea to flaunt expensive, state-of-the-art technical equipment at an AGM. It may be necessary to use some fairly sophisticated presentation technology if the audience is large or the subject matter calls for it, but shareholders are usually conscious that the money you are spending is theirs and if you appear to be spending too much of it the law of diminishing returns sets in.

More than at any other conference event, the AGM should use technology to support speakers rather than supplant them. This support may simply be in the form of well-designed slides or video sequences showing financial information, or it could involve more sophisticated technology like interactive video disks designed to give platform speakers instant access to information with which to answer shareholder's questions. But, at all times, the technology should play second fiddle to the people who matter at this event – the speakers.

THE ROAD SHOW

A road show is an event that can travel to a number of different venues. Sometimes the success of a major event in a prime location results in a cut-down version being staged in other locations later; and some road shows are planned from the start as events to be mounted in a variety of locations, all of which are equally important.

The effective road show

The effectiveness of a road show depends to a large extent on what you can pack into a lorry. A large show, designed and created for a spacious exhibition centre or conference venue, will rarely transfer well to a number of different smaller halls, unless very detailed planning has taken place right from the start. Simply taking the main elements of the show and packing them off to a different location that's smaller and less well equipped invites disappointment; essential features will be missing and the impact will almost certainly be considerably less than originally achieved.

But if the requirement for a road show is known at the planning stage of the main event, it's a relatively easy matter to design and create both events in tandem. A modular approach is usually adopted, allowing elements of the main show to be incorporated in a road show. This may take on a slightly different form, but it will be created to make the best and most effective use of the existing elements of the main show, so providing a far more impressive touring version.

Creative content

Producing a road show specifically to tour a number of different venues is first of all about creative content. Will the show appeal to all its intended audiences? Will it achieve its objectives? After that, it's primarily a matter of logistics and cost. What's the size of the smallest venue, in contrast to the size of the largest? What facilities exist? When are the venues available? Answers to these questions will help you arrive at a blueprint for the design and content of the show, and will also enable you to estimate the costs of such essentials as set, personality presenters, transport and crew.

Road show resources

The road show is an excellent way to take a company's message to a variety of different audiences. But an effective, trouble-free road show is usually the result of a great deal of expert planning and organisation, and this is perhaps best left to specialist presentation companies. By all means involve your company personnel in the planning stages to make sure the right messages are being communicated in the right way. But unless you're prepared for them to devote much of their time to planning a road show schedule, booking venues, hiring crews, organising transport and so on – activities in which they're probably not experienced – leave these matters to one of the many specialist conference companies. Use their resources to ensure your image is presented effectively and with impact; use your own to do what it is your company does best.

THE PRODUCT LAUNCH

The product launch can be pure showbusiness, creating an exciting, glamorous environment in which the new product is featured as the star of the show. Or it can be a more low-key affair, introducing a product to an audience more interested in its technical performance than its sales potential.

Techniques

Many 'showbusiness' product launches use an impressive array of techniques to create stunning effects. Huge sets, complex lighting rigs, multi-screen video or slide presentations, dry ice, stereo sound and effects – all are frequently used to mount product launches which are often 'fronted' by a personality presenter, perhaps assisted by a supporting cast of actors, actresses and the obligatory chorus of showgirls.

It goes without saying that these events can be expensive; but if buyers in your intended market have been conditioned to expect product launches of this kind it becomes difficult to break the mould and risk exposing your product and your company to the charge of penny-pinching. It is possible, however, to

minimise the expense while keeping entertainment values high
The use of an unusual, even eccentric, venue can often contribute a great deal to the memorability of a product launch; and
constructing the event around a more expensive – but more
charismatic – presenter might also allow cost savings to be made
in other areas (see Chapter 3 for more details).

A cost saving that should not be contemplated, however, is to
attempt the planning and execution of such an event without at
least the assistance of a reputable specialist production company
(see list on pages 196–199 of this book). Although some types of
conference activity can be undertaken without employing
specialists, it's generally true that this is not one of them. The
'showbusiness' product launch demands great expertise, a
special kind of creativity, and access to a vast range of specialised
techniques and technicians, all of which are unlikely to be found
within most business organisations.

Audiences

The launch of a product to a more 'technical' audience can be far
less showy, far less expensive and may even be straightforward
enough to be produced in-house. There is a strong argument for
avoiding any display of conspicuous expenditure with these
events; audiences for them tend to consider product development more important than product promotion.

A technically-minded audience usually wants to see the product and to see it in operation. The event should therefore be
constructed around this requirement, with visual support material clearly demonstrating the product's capabilities and a
number of specimen products made available for demonstration
or for members of the audience to examine or operate.

Presentation

In general, sets for these 'technical' product launches should be
simple yet effective: visual support material – slides, video etc. –
should concentrate on the product's technical merits avoiding
elaborate visual effects and, if a personality presenter is used,
care should be taken to choose someone with at least a little

experience of presenting similar events. There are not many professional presenters around who can strike the delicate balance between efficiently presenting themselves and effectively presenting a product to a technically-oriented audience.

SPECIAL EVENT PRODUCTIONS

Planning, organising and executing corporate special events are activities very often performed by specialist agencies or PR companies. The nature of these events varies greatly – anything from a sponsored walk in aid of a local charity to a lavishly-mounted Elizabethan banquet – but their objectives are similar; usually to promote the image of a company and/or its products.

Who is responsible?

As with the more flamboyant forms of product launch it is advisable to use specialists to handle most, if not all, of the work involved in mounting a special event. The original idea for such an event may well come from within your company, however, and providing it makes commercial sense, is practicable and within the allocated budget the specialist agency you choose may be restricted simply to carrying out your creative plan. There is a danger here, however; although creative ideas conceived 'in-house' often work well because their creators are far more aware of the composition and nature of the intended audience than any outside agency, it is all too easy to seize upon ideas which have outlived their usefulness. There is a fashion season for ideas as much as for clothing and one of the advantages of employing a good specialist agency is that it will be aware of what fashion is 'in' and what's 'out' – and come up with an idea that borrows just enough from current fashion to make it comfortable, but with a creative twist that can also make it memorable and exciting.

PR aspects

Many special events can attract a great deal of media attention – an aspect that should be weighed in the balance when assessing the potential benefits such events can bring. Once again, it is advisable to employ a specialist PR agency to maximise the effectiveness of media coverage and, although this will add to overall costs, it may be well worth while if achieving a high PR profile is one of the objectives of the event.

EXHIBITIONS

Given that the primary objective of most of the conference events outlined above is to convey a message to an audience, every opportunity should be taken to achieve that objective – which may well mean considering the benefits offered by mounting an exhibition associated with the main event.

Space utilisation

Whatever the size and expense of the venue hired to mount the main event, full use of all the available space makes good sense, and impressive or informative displays can often be mounted in quite small areas. At most AGMs, for example, there is usually a refreshment area for shareholders in which space can easily be found for a display of a company's current activities. Similarly, when the subject of a conference is a new product or technique, reception or refreshment areas can be used very effectively to display relevant material. In some cases – where the product is very large or the technique quite complex – the use of an associated exhibition area may prove particularly useful; it may be difficult to convey the size, impressiveness or complexity of a subject in the main presentation area because of space or distance limitations, so it makes sense to give delegates an opportunity to 'see for themselves' in a nearby exhibition area.

Exhibition design

Design is an important exhibition consideration. Even the very smallest exhibit, perhaps consisting of little more than a few captioned photographs on stand-alone panels, while not necessarily needing the services of a designer should be prepared and executed with care. At a recent product launch by a well-known photographic company, a small exhibition area featured a number of display panels bearing badly-photographed and enlarged product shots, one of which even bore the much-enlarged imprint of a photographic technician's thumb! The audience for the event consisted of professional film makers, people who demand the highest quality standards from manufacturers who supply the products they use. Needless to say, they were not impressed.

For larger exhibitions associated with other events, wherever possible the same designer should be used to create both the main event and the exhibition to ensure continuity of style. The overall design of an event can have a great effect on an audience and when a great deal of thought has gone into devising a suitable design style for the main event an exhibition area in a totally different – or even subtly different – style could be dangerously ineffective.

Objectives

But any exhibition, large or small, associated with another event should be treated as an integral part of the main event and not simply 'stuck on' to use up space or because some photographs happen to be available. Like any other form of conference activity, an exhibition should be planned and executed to achieve a specific objective; if the main event can achieve that objective then there's probably no need for an associated exhibition. You might ask the question: 'Does the audience need information it may not be possible to convey during the main event?' If the answer is 'Yes' then an exhibition running alongside the main event could well provide the solution.

SEMINARS AND SYMPOSIA

The objective of any group holding a discussion or meeting to exchange information is to concentrate on the business in hand; the role of the organiser in this instance is therefore not to create a presentation but to create the conditions in which others may do so.

Special attention must therefore be paid to technical and administrative arrangements if the event is to run smoothly and effectively. The most complimentary thing that can be said after a successful seminar is that no one noticed the organisation.

Technical considerations

Although it is unlikely these events will require complex technical equipment, it is especially important that whatever equipment is required is thoroughly checked, particularly if the venue is supplying it. In general – although there are honourable exceptions – equipment held by conference venues should be treated as highly suspect. Don't take the venue equipment list for granted – ask to see the equipment, get it out, check it thoroughly, hold a full-scale rehearsal if at all possible – all the time remembering the old conference adage 'If it can go wrong, it will'. Have a 'Plan B' for when things do go wrong, even if it's only to take an extra projector lamp along with you on the day. The availability or otherwise of spare projector lamps, incidentally, is an excellent test of the venue's technical capability.

Organisation

Organising seminars and similar events can be a problem if the participants are uncooperative or simply unavailable. Businesspeople usually present no difficulties in this respect, but academics and scientists are notoriously difficult to pin down and it's often well worth while paying extra attention to detail in these cases. This can simply mean agreeing a schedule with all concerned at the early planning stage, establishing a number of clearly defined key dates – for delivery of scripts, visual material etc. – then keeping everyone involved fully informed of the event's progress at regular intervals, and in writing.

These are procedures which should be followed with most events, but they are particularly important if there's the slightest risk that some or all of the necessary material will not arrive on schedule. Should this happen and the event suffers as a result, the organiser will naturally be held solely responsible – although, conversely, the organiser of a successful seminar or symposium should not expect thanks!

TRAINING

Many presentational techniques used in the categories mentioned above can be used when groups of people meet for training. It might be more accurate to say 'should be used' for all too often training sessions concentrate on imparting information without paying too much attention to the needs of trainees or students. In common with every other audience, students are being given a message, and in order to convey that message clearly and effectively it is advisable to give some thought to the way in which the message is packaged and presented.

Techniques

Technically, almost all the aids available to conference producers can be used in the training room. Used conventionally, video, slide/tape, overhead projectors and print can all form valuable parts of a training package. But training packages, unlike most conferences, are often given in more controllable conditions and usually repeated many times so it becomes possible – and economically feasible – to use a number of less conventional technical aids.

Interactive video gives students the opportunity of reacting to situations or questions presented to them, often in a 'real life' form, on a video screen. Originally, interactive videos were played to students from tape, allowing only a sequential path to be followed, but with the video disk, produced from a conventionally-shot videotape original, a random access system gives students the ability to follow a number of different information or learning paths, depending upon each students' learning capacity. Although interactive video disks are still relatively expensive to produce and are therefore best suited to training a number of different groups over a fairly long time-span, they can offer many benefits. Trainers welcome the wide range and depth of information such systems can deliver, while students often find that controlling their own learning pace makes the learning process more enjoyable and far more successful.

The computer offers similar interactive possibilities and many programs are now available to train staff in a variety of skills from typing to senior management. The modern computer – small, self-contained, incredibly powerful and capable of displaying on screen a vast number of visual effects, from simple animated charts to 'live action' video material – has the potential to revolutionise training; but in this field it is – or should be – essentially a 'one-to-one' medium and therefore falls outside the scope of this book. However, for a brief survey of the uses of the computer as an interactive medium in conference presentation and as a source of graphics, see Chapter 10.

TELECONFERENCING

On a television news programme recently the studio newscaster in London calmly conducted a 'live' interview with an expedition leader whom we saw standing half-way up a mountain in the Himalayas. The pictures were crystal clear, the sound quality perfect; and the technology used to make this news item not only possible but increasingly routine also regularly brings together businesspeople all over the world through the television medium.

Technology

Early attempts at teleconferencing (also called videoconferencing) were not always successful. The technologies used were still new and untried, and landline connections could be unreliable. In the past few years, however, television technology has progressed by leaps and bounds; cameras, for example, are now extremely reliable, far smaller and much more sensitive, needing very little light to capture a good quality picture. More important, communications satellites have made the transmission of television pictures and sound to and from almost anywhere in the world an everyday occurrence, one we are beginning to be able to take for granted.

Applications

Teleconferencing has obvious advantages where groups of people in a number of widely-spaced locations wish to hold a meeting without spending a great deal of time and money travelling to a single location. Engineers or scientists can use it to demonstrate progress or problems to colleagues on the other side of the world; an international salesforce can attend a worldwide sales conference; and the medium might also be used as part of a conventional conference event to carry contributions from guest speakers who may be too distant, busy or expensive to invite in person.

Teleconferencing is still a fairly expensive medium; but with an increasing number of communications satellites in orbit and further improvements in landline technology being made we are beginning to see much greater competition between communications companies so it may well become a more economic proposition in the near future.

Despite its advantages for international companies with key staff situated in many different locations, it's doubtful whether the teleconference can ever replace the conventional conference event, however. It's been said that a great deal of the real work at a conventional conference takes place either before or after the main event – and usually in the bar. There is a social aspect to a 'live' conference that television cannot hope to match and although teleconferencing is predicted to gain in popularity there is an artificiality about it that, according to some, will always put it in second place behind a real, 'live' event. But, undeniably, teleconferencing does provide perhaps the most cost-effective method yet developed for arranging a meeting between the far-flung representatives of international companies – and with an increasing number of companies operating globally, teleconferencing looks set for a secure future.

For more information on teleconferencing, see Chapter 10.

2 Planning

- What type of conference? • What style of production? • Where will you hold the event?
- The budget • Appointing a producer • The producer's role • The client's role • Scheduling • Security

There's no mystery about conference planning once you decide exactly what it is you intend to do. Put very simply, it's a matter of knowing what sort of event you want to hold, how and where you want to hold it, and who will be responsible for its various aspects.

Once those decisions have been made the creative side of the event can be planned – but beware of reversing the procedure and trying to fit everything around a good creative idea. There's no harm in thinking about creative ideas at this stage, but it's far more important to lay the ground rules of the event first. Once that's done, it's surprising how often the process of thinking the event through produces a number of other ideas which are not only more practical than your first thoughts, but frequently much better.

WHAT TYPE OF CONFERENCE?

So first you need to be sure what type of conference you are planning. The definitions given in Chapter 1 should give some guide to this, but if you're in doubt the following checklist could help you identify the kind of event you're about to plan.

● *Who is your target audience?*

Identify them. Are they salespeople, office staff, potential clients, existing customers, the general public?

● *What is the primary objective of your event?*

What single message should your audience take away from the event? For example, are you asking them to sell more products, to deliver a better service, to understand a new working method or technique, or to take credit for their past efforts?

● *What secondary messages could or should be conveyed?*

For example, this might be a good opportunity to promote details of changes or additions to products or services, to talk about personnel changes or to discuss information on the activities of your competitors.

● *Where is your event to be held?*

This will depend upon a number of factors, such as the size of the target audience, the facilities needed and venue availability. See Chapter 4 for more information on venues.

● *What's the size of your budget?*

A meagre budget may affect your choice of venue or make a lavish production impossible; but a really good idea, well executed, can make even the most inexpensive event memorable.

Identifying the primary objective will almost certainly point to the type of event you're planning to produce – and what's more, clearly fixing that primary objective in your mind now will enable you to focus more clearly on the production values and creative input necessary to make the event both productive and successful.

Note that it's the identification of the *primary* conference objective that's most important; any number of secondary objectives may be desired, but never forget that they are secondary. The event you're planning is going to cost your company money – a considerable amount if it's a large conference – so it's essential that when it's over the audience leaves with your primary message firmly in mind. But don't try to get 'good value for money' by trying to cram everything in all at once; motivating a salesforce, explaining a new corporate structure and describing company progress throughout the year will not only add to the complexity and cost of the event – it will almost certainly leave the audience bewildered by the amount of information they've been asked to assimilate. And bewilderment is not an ideal audience reaction.

WHAT STYLE OF PRODUCTION?

With your primary objective set and the type of conference you are planning decided, the next issue to consider is the production style.

The subject matter will shape the style to a certain extent, and in addition the composition and nature of the audience should provide another valuable guide to the style you might adopt. As a general rule, style should follow content – a conference for chartered accountants on new accounting procedures should be businesslike, a salesforce conference might be spectacular, inspirational – but some of the most successful conferences have broken this rule and succeeded in delivering messages to their audiences using the most unlikely styles. Here are just two examples.

A major UK food company planned to hold a sales conference somewhere in the Midlands. The company had enjoyed a successful year and wanted to congratulate its salesforce while setting even higher targets for the year to come.

Stratford upon Avon was chosen as the venue and *As You Like It* as the conference theme, with the Shade of Shakespeare (excellently portrayed by Ron Moody) delivering a light-hearted Shakespearean 'send-up' written entirely in blank verse. Despite early fears that this approach might lack the 'popular' touch, the conference was a great success and two years later was still remembered by its salesforce audience.

An insurance company launching a new product to brokers saw the need to stress the company's long record of success in the insurance market.

The event took the form of a 'Journey Into The Past', with the venue, the set and much of the presentation material used conjuring up bygone days – when naturally the insurance company involved was as much of a household name as it is today. The opening 12-minute audio-visual presentation on this theme was later produced as a sales aid for brokers, in which form it won a major award from the British Industrial and Scientific Film Association.

If there is anything to be learned from these two examples it is that if you want your audience to do something, give them something in return – in these cases it was entertainment. Don't give them too much though; many well-meaning producers have presided over events in which the conference message has sunk so deeply into a surrounding wash of frothy entertainment that it has been swamped entirely. But although the line is a tricky one to tread, it is far better to aim for something unusual, unexpected – always bearing in mind the primary objective of the event – than to succumb to the lure of 'doing it like last year' simply because no one actually walked out. Remember, your conference audience will often be there because they are told to be there; but even though they can be ordered to see the presentation, they can't be ordered to remember it.

A long-serving conference producer once remarked, 'You've got 200 people sitting in a room waiting for a conference to start. And usually all of them have just one thought in their minds – what time does the bar open!' Choosing a different, perhaps off-beat style of presentation could very well take your audience's minds away from opening time and on to the matter in hand.

WHERE WILL YOU HOLD THE EVENT?

The choice of venue is vitally important; the right venue can add a great deal to the success of an event, while the wrong one can destroy it. Good venues are in great demand, however, so there's something to be said for beginning your search for a venue as early in the planning stage as you can. But see Chapter 4 for more on venues.

THE BUDGET

Although it may seem too obvious to mention, budgeting really should be clearly distinguished from costing. A budget is the amount you are prepared to spend; a costing is what you may have to pay. But once these differences are understood, it should make 'overspending the budget' a phrase you should never need to use. Get the costing right and, so long as the sum arrived at is within the budget, it should be impossible to overspend. Always excepting unforeseen circumstances, of course!

A cost estimate

Costing a large or technically complex conference is a specialist's job; there are usually so many elements to be taken into consideration when such a costing is prepared it would be a sensible precaution to tread very warily around any figures produced by a non-specialist. But for a fairly straightforward event you should be able to produce a reasonably accurate cost estimate even without a specialist's knowledge. By the time the budgeting stage has been reached you should know when and where the event is taking place and have a detailed outline of its content; armed with this information the event can be broken down into its constituent parts using a costing form similar to the example on pages 38–9.

The form is typical of the kind used by specialist conference production companies and it contains items the organiser using in-house resources won't necessarily have to pay for directly. For example, venue research and booking, scriptwriting and preparing slides are just three jobs that could be done by in-house personnel. But beware – these services are not free! If company staff are asked to do these jobs, their time needs to be costed, because there's no doubt it will cost your company money. In-house work on the conference will take up a certain percentage of staff time and that percentage should appear – in monetary terms – against the relevant activity in the costing form. And don't underestimate how long your staff might need to do some of these unfamiliar jobs. Take scriptwriting for example. After some years at the job I'm somewhat surprised to find it still takes me an average of one hour to write one minute of conference script. That's a 'theatrical' presentation; a more conventional event takes less time to write, but I reckon a newcomer to the business would be doing well to produce a good first draft script of a simple hour-long conference in two to three days.

One more point should be made about the sample form given here. There's no such thing as a 'typical' conference, so the form should not be thought of as complete; your conference may well have many additional items which will need costing.

Checking the estimate

If you've had little or no experience of costing a conference it might be a good idea to get a second opinion on your cost estimate. One way to do this is to go to someone in your accounts department, take a little time to explain the nature of the event and then ask for your estimate to be checked. It's surprising how often a coldly analytical – and uninvolved – eye can spot a glaring error or omission that someone closer to the event has over-looked.

Alternatively, you might telephone a few conference production companies, describe the event being prepared, mention a budget – the result of your costing – and note the reaction. This might be considered a little unfair to the production companies you ring, who aren't in business to provide free budgetary advice to people who are trying to go it alone. But the contact could be of benefit to both parties; you might well find that talking to an expert provides useful information, while the production company contacted, if it's good at its job – and most are – will take your name and make a follow-up call a few days or weeks later. If that call coincides with a moment when you've hit a problem then you could be grateful for their help; but even if it doesn't

CONFERENCE ESTIMATE

ONE. PRE-PRODUCTION

Briefings/meetings (writer/designer/director)	———
Research/recces/planning	———
Design work	———
Scriptwriting (3 drafts)	———
Design/script presentation	———
Travel/expenses	———
SUB TOTAL	———

TWO: CONFERENCE PRODUCTION

VENUE: Research and recce ———
Venue hire ———
Set construction and materials ———
Lighting (inc. staff, recce, rig & operation) ———
Sound (inc. staff, recce, rig & operation) ———
Equipment hire – 'bought-in' AV ———
Equipment hire – 'bought-in' video ———
Miscellaneous facilities ———
Transport hire ———
Tech. crew: crew @   hr ×   hrs ———
Crew accommodation ———
Direction (inc. rehearsals) ———

AV PRODUCTION: (briefing, direction & production) ———
AV equipment hire (inc. transport) ———
AV crew hire (inc. accommodation and travel) ———

VIDEO PRODUCTION: (briefing, writing, directing) ———
Video shoot: (days @   day) ———
Travel costs (road/rail/air) ———
Accommodation expenses ———
Editing/post prod: hrs @   hr + FX ———
Studio hire: days @   day ———
Artiste/presenter fee (v.o. fee) ———
Make-up ———
Equipment hire ———
Stock ———
Video pres. equipt: (monitors, proj. etc.) GE proj. ———
Technical crew (inc. accommodation) ———
Incidentals (postage/phone/meetings etc.) ———

EVENT PRODUCTION: (research/selection) _____

Event artistes audition/rehearsal _____

Event artiste fees _____

Event direction (inc. client rehearsal) _____

Event venue or facility fee (boat hire) _____

Tech. crew: crew @ hr × hrs _____

Equipment/facilities (on-board entertainment) _____

PRINT: Briefing and design _____

Print production _____

Signage/graphics _____

SUB TOTAL _____

THREE: MISCELLANEOUS SERVICES

Autocue/portaprompt/QTV (+ operator) _____

Stills photography _____

Secretarial services _____

Office equipment hire (fax/WP/copier) _____

Music selection (library) _____

Copyright on music/visuals _____

Conference presenter (intro and links only) _____

Translation fees _____

Supply translators _____

Translation equipment _____

Edit music/sound tapes _____

Preparing master video and txfr to cassette _____

Duplication: copies of VHS/Beta/U-Matic @ each: _____

Producer's fee _____

Incidentals (postage/phone/meetings) _____

Preview: equipment/staff/transport etc. _____

Technical services (line booking etc.) _____

SUB TOTAL _____

TOTAL OF ONE + TWO + THREE _____

+ 10% CONTINGENCY _____

TOTAL _____

+ VAT @ 17.5% _____

TOTAL _____

lead to immediate work that call could be the start of a relationship which might bear fruit at a later date.

Budgeting responsibilities

Setting a budget and making sure the costing matches it are
really two separate jobs and ought to be undertaken by two
different people. There's no problem when a production company is involved; the client sets the budget, the production
company's costing must meet it. But when both the budget and
the costing are being handled 'in-house' – possibly even by the
same person – it can happen that the figures are unreliable, not
only possibly due to inexperience but also because the pressure
that exists in the client/production house relationship is absent.

One answer to this problem is to identify the key individual in
the company who has overall responsibility for the event, then
create an 'in-house' production group responding to that individual as if he or she were an outside company. Setting up such
a group can be a most effective way of handling an event
'in-house' – and it will pay particular dividends at the
costing/budgeting stage, keeping the 'client' separate from the
'production team' personnel who will then be more likely to
produce realistic figures.

APPOINTING A PRODUCER

Do you appoint a producer and a production team from outside
your company or do you select a producer and team from
members of your own staff? The answer depends upon the size
and complexity of the event being planned, the abilities of your
staff and their availability.

The in-house organiser who has had little or no experience of
larger, more complex events would be wise to select a professional production team from one of the many operating in this
field. (For a list of conference production companies see pages
196–199.) Such a team will have information resources your own
staff may have difficulty in finding; it will have access to
specialised knowledge and skills rarely available to those outside
the conference industry; and, most important, it can devote all
its time and effort to producing your event.

Selecting an in-house production team

If you do decide to appoint 'in-house' production personnel, it is important to recruit them from the right levels from within your organisation and to be sure they are capable of doing the job. Questions to ask at this stage might include the following.

YOUR PRODUCTION TEAM

- *Is the team leader – the producer – able to command respect?*

- *Is the producer able to motivate others?*

- *Does the producer have sufficient technical knowledge of the conference medium?*

- *Is the producer aware of the conference objectives and in broad agreement with the means you intend to adopt to achieve them?*

- *Will the producer be able to devote sufficient time to planning and producing the event?*

- *Have the other members of the production team been selected for the talents they can bring to the project – or simply because they are underemployed?*

- *Are you prepared to reallocate the work of some or all of the staff selected to join the production team?*

- *Do all the members of the production team work well together under pressure?*

- *Does everyone understand that there will almost certainly be a need to work late and perhaps at weekends?*

THE PRODUCER'S ROLE

By selecting and appointing a producer for your event, you will be asking someone to take full responsibility for its success or failure. Now that's a great deal of power to hand over to anyone, so it would be advisable to choose a producer with care and with at least a little knowledge of what you can expect from that person – and what the producer will be expecting from you.

So what does a conference producer actually do?

- The producer is responsible to the client for both the logistic and creative aspects of the event.

- Logistically, the producer will supervise and co-ordinate all the elements that go towards the event's creation.

- The producer will draw up a master schedule for the event and take overall responsibility for its implementation.

- The producer may delegate the production of some elements of the event – AV or video sections for example – to others, but the producer alone is responsible for their quality and timely delivery.

- The producer has obligations to work within an agreed budget and time-scale, to observe legal requirements (copyright, per-forming rights, AGM procedures etc.) and to keep the client fully informed of the progress of the event.

The producer and creativity

Creatively, the producer's position is a little less straight-forward. As the person ultimately responsible for ensuring that the client's message is successfully conveyed and understood, it follows that in theory the conference producer should have the final say in determining how that message should be presented – its creative style. As the expert in communication, the argument goes, the producer's creative ideas should be paramount. In practice, however, the client must have the final creative say, if only because it is the client who is footing the bill.

In the majority of cases a happy creative balance can be struck between client and producer, but if a producer violently dis-agrees with the client's creative input two courses of action are open. The choice is either resign; or carry on, performing the necessary duties totally professionally, in the same way that barristers diligently defend clients they know are guilty. As neither of these alternatives is ideal (although the second has resulted in some surprisingly successful events), it is vitally important that client and producer establish some form of creative rapport in the early stages of the event – preferably when the client briefs the producer at the initial production meeting.

The producer's creative role then, is primarily to reach an amicable agreement with the client on the creative style of the event before the production process begins. Once this has been done, the producer will be responsible for ensuring the event takes place in the agreed style and to the highest possible standard of quality – a responsibility which may involve a variety of disciplines such as set design, stage lighting, scriptwriting, sound recording, direction and many more. There will almost certainly be disagreements on detail as the event takes shape, but if a firm understanding has been established between client and producer in the vital early stages, these should not be insurmountable.

THE CLIENT'S ROLE

The partnership between client and producer should be – and often is – enjoyable, constructive and ultimately fruitful. The producer brings specialised knowledge and abilities to that partnership – but what is the greatest contribution a client can make?

The answer, in a word, is clarity. Clients who know precisely what they want their event to achieve and exactly how much they have to spend will be welcomed with a sigh of relief by any producer, whether 'in-house' or appointed from an outside production company.

A clear, concise brief, delivered by the person who conceived it, immediately establishes a good relationship, giving the production team a sharply-focused picture of the size and shape of the task ahead. (See page 87 for a description of the briefing process.)

Communicating with the team

When the production process begins, the client can do much to smooth its path by establishing good communications between the client company and the production team. One point of contact within the company is best – call that person the executive producer to make up for all the extra work involved – and it will be the executive producer's task to ensure the schedule is observed within the company and that all relevant company personnel are being kept informed (and chased) on deadlines for scripts or other material.

Busy executives don't have a great deal of time to spare, so it's unrealistic to expect them to devote much energy to preparing for an event which may still be a few months away. But if the production team is to do the best possible job for your company, an efficient and speedy communication link is essential. It's worth bearing in mind that professional conference companies often work unusual hours so giving your production company the home telephone number of your executive producer could be invaluable to them – if not quite so welcome to your producer.

And whether you employ an outside production house or choose an 'in-house' production team, remember they're on your side and give them encouragement. Putting together a conference can be a frustrating affair at times and, by showing enthusiasm, interest and involvement, a client can generate a great deal of goodwill within the production team, encouraging them to produce even better work.

Scheduling

The producers, craftspeople and technicians working in the conference field can and often do work miracles, delivering scripts, sets and even complete presentations incredibly quickly. Whether their work is as good as it might be if given a reasonable time in which to complete it is another matter.

Deadlines

Almost everyone working in the conference industry has horrific tales to tell of impossible deadlines, scripts hastily written in hotel bedrooms, hurriedly-constructed sets held together with sticky tape and nailed into place, and the slide show no one has seen until the managing director presses the button to begin it. It would be nice to think it's all unavoidable, but somehow these stories continue to circulate with production crews reporting new and ever more amazing cliff-hanging exploits. Perhaps it's to be expected. Conferences can be like theatrical productions – a kind of controlled frenzy takes hold of everyone as the 'first night' approaches, and those elegant plans and schedules drawn up weeks ago seem somehow to get forgotten. A conference can be even worse than a theatrical production, for the 'first night' is usually also the last – you get one chance to get it right in front of an audience and no more.

Good scheduling gives you a chance to set your deadlines in advance so you arrive at the performance of your event – be it a full-scale conference or AGM, or a small group meeting or seminar – with as few worries as possible. If all the activities associated with your event have been scheduled correctly – and if everyone involved has worked to the schedule deadlines – then all you have to worry about is the performance itself. Which is usually enough.

The agency producer

Who should be responsible for drawing up the schedule and ensuring it is carried out on time? The short answer is the producer.

If a conference production house is handling the event for you then this task can safely be left to the producer appointed by the company you are using. Remember though, that producer is in a tricky position; there is no desire to antagonise you – the client – but the producer may have to insist quite strongly on certain deadlines being met by you and by members of your staff – the writing of speeches or the supply of information or artwork for slides for example. It's the producer who carries the can if things go wrong; if the event's a disaster the production company will not be invited back to work for you again, so it has a vested interest in ensuring its success. If you, too, want it to be a success, then there should be no problem in co-operating fully with the producer and ensuring other members of your staff do the same.

The in-house producer

By appointing a producer you are effectively handing over much of the responsibility for the event to that person – and with that responsibility must go a certain amount of power. This can lead to difficulties when the event is being handled 'in-house' for the staff member designated as producer must be given the same power and responsibility as the professional appointed by the production house. The professional has the advantage of being outside your company and can therefore speak (politely, one hopes) to staff at all levels. The 'in-house' producer may be junior in rank to some of the conference participants and could find it difficult to bully them for material – and make no mistake, bullying will be needed at times.

If you are appointing a fairly junior staff member as producer, make it quite clear to everyone – up to and including the managing director and/or Chief Executive – that the person concerned is assuming a great responsibility on behalf of the company and deserves everyone's full co-operation.

Incidentally, it should be noted that a common characteristic of many professional conference producers is their ability to get along with a wide range of different people; if you are appointing a member of your staff to fulfil this role, make sure he or she has a similar ability.

A schedule blueprint

If a professional producer is handling the event the scheduling will be carried out by the production house – and slavishly followed by you. If you are handling the event 'in-house' you will need to tackle the scheduling yourself or delegate it to a colleague who, from the moment the date of the event is fixed, will begin compiling a master schedule enabling progress of each part of the event to be monitored.

Although all events are made up of different elements and therefore have different scheduling requirements, here are a few typical questions to help get the scheduling process under way. I'll assume the nature and content of the event are known in sufficient detail to enable the process of scheduling to begin, but would advise you *not* to do the same. Always ensure that a fairly firm ground plan for the event exists before drawing up your schedule, or it will mean nothing.

After each of these questions, the name of the person responsible for taking appropriate action by a stated date should be added.

SCHEDULING QUESTIONS

Activity	Action

1. Has the venue been booked and a deposit paid?

NAME _____

DATE _____

2. Have speakers been briefed and delivery dates set for scripts and visual support material?

NAME _____

DATE _____

3. Has equipment been booked, ordered and checked? If 'in-house' equipment is to be used, has it been checked?

NAME _____

DATE _____

4. Is printed material needed? If so, check deadline dates with writer/designer/printer.

NAME _____

DATE _____

5. Are invitations to be sent? A mailing list will be needed and a mailing date determined.

NAME _____

DATE _____

6. Is a 'set' or some form of set dressing required? Who designs it, supplies it and how much time will be required to produce it?

NAME _____

DATE _____

box continues ▶

Activity	Action
7. Book rehearsal space. Check with venue to discover availability for dress rehearsal before main event.	NAME_____ DATE_____
8. Are transport arrangements necessary? Have they been made?	NAME_____ DATE_____
9. Does the event require press coverage? Have journalists been contacted?	NAME_____ DATE_____
10. Is slide/tape, video or film included in the event? Does this material need to be produced? Have delivery dates been set?	NAME_____ DATE_____
11. Have arrangements been made to circulate updated schedules regularly to all concerned?	NAME_____ DATE_____

These are the bare bones of a schedule, merely the start of a process which branches out into any number of subdivisions as each constituent part of the event is activated. Separate schedules will be required for many of the activities listed above. The production of an AV or video, for example, will need to take into account the time required to write and receive approval of an outline and a full script; to book crews and artists; to shoot and edit the material; to record a commentary; and to preview the finished programme, allowing time to make changes if necessary. Similarly, the event itself will need to be scheduled, from the moment the venue becomes available to the time when the delegates leave, and the set and equipment must be cleared.

A detailed and accurate master schedule incorporating all these different but interlocking elements is essential if an event is to be successful. The computer is an extremely useful tool in this respect, allowing organisers to construct a simple model of the event in which each element has its own planning and scheduling 'area' interacting with others. If the software you are currently using offers 'outlining' or similar facilities it will be easy to construct a schedule in this way and the guide below shows the constituent parts of a typical master schedule for an event produced by an in-house team. Planned with care and implemented diligently – and with a certain amount of persistence – the existence of such a schedule generates a feeling of confidence not only among the members of the production team, but also among everyone associated with the event. A good schedule tells them you know where you're going.

MASTER SCHEDULE

Planning meetings

Selecting/briefing production team

Brief writer – script/edit contributors' texts

Visual material – collate, commission artwork

• Venue	• Transport	• Print	• Set/signage	• AV/slides	• Video
Recce	Quotes	Invites	Design	Commission	Shoot
Book	Visit	Literature	Build	Shoot	Edit
Liaise	Book	Design	Install	Preview	Preview

Book technical facilities – book artistes/speakers

PR – invitations – press releases

Rehearsals (run-throughs)

Venue dress rehearsal

Event!

SECURITY

Apart from the question of physical security at the chosen location (see Chapter 4), many events feature the discussion of sensitive commercial information which must also be protected. I once worked on a major conference for a large UK chemical company launching an important new product to the salesforce. After some weeks' work on the project and about three days before the event, a rival company announced the launch of a similar product with an almost identical name. There had obviously been an information leak. The production team immediately fell under suspicion and, for a while, the atmosphere became extremely tense; the client began making thinly-veiled accusations concerning our trustworthiness and we found it difficult to protest our innocence when we, as 'outsiders', knew how important the new product was and how much it was potentially worth to a commercial rival. But then one of the company's own senior staff was revealed as the 'mole' when he suddenly accepted a highly-paid job for the rival company and we were exonerated – but it was a most unpleasant experience for us all.

For the duration of the production the producer – and perhaps many members of the production team – will be working closely with the client's company and may have access to sensitive commercial information. Some companies consider it necessary to ask outside suppliers to sign an agreement guaranteeing the security of such information. In practice, however, this precaution is rarely necessary; even the suspicion of a 'leak' traceable to a conference production company would make it very difficult, if not impossible, for that company to operate in the conference field again. All reputable production companies, therefore, will invariably keep confidential information totally secure.

3 CREATING THE CONCEPT

- The first production meeting ● The brief
- The concept ● Ideas – and how to get them
- The second production meeting

THE FIRST PRODUCTION MEETING

You may have decided to use an outside production house to handle your event, or you may have selected an in-house team and decided to go it alone, but now is the time to meet the people who will be helping you put your event together – your production team.

The first time you meet your entire production team gives you an ideal opportunity to establish the basis of a good working relationship, so allow plenty of time for this meeting and try to ensure there are no interruptions. The 'working lunch' is often derided, but at least no office phones are ringing and the atmosphere is likely to be more informal, with ideas tending to flow much more freely.

The initial production meeting will normally be held on your own ground – at your office or headquarters – and it will be useful if all the people who will be speaking at the event can make at least a token appearance to meet the producer and the team, however briefly. Apart from the natural courtesy of this arrangement, it gives the production team a good idea of any special assistance the speakers may require. Someone with a particularly soft voice, for example, may need extra amplification for a large audience.

If the team you're meeting for the first time comes from a production house there should be no need for their producer to talk about money, apart from how the budget is to be allocated, still less to remind the client tactfully that the first stage payment is overdue. All financial arrangements should have been made when the production company was appointed and, just as the client expects the production company to fulfil its part of the bargain, so does the production company expect to be paid according to the agreed terms. Late payments can sour a good working relationship; no one likes to ask for money, particularly a producer attempting to form a close partnership with a client.

The agenda for the initial production meeting should be constructed so that when the meeting ends everyone present will have agreed the following.

1. A draft working schedule. The person who will be responsible for the master schedule should also have been identified.

2. The identity of the key company contact – the executive producer.

3. The identities and duties of an 'in-house' production team where appropriate.

4. An action plan for progressing any special requirements – such as AV or video, guest speakers, exhibition units etc.

5. A draft creative approach – a concept – where this is necessary.

6. A date and an agenda for the next meeting.

All these points are important – but perhaps none more so than number five. This is the one that will set the style and tone of your event – the concept around which the event will be developed.

THE BRIEF

If you're asking people – whether an in-house team or an outside agency – to come up with a concept for your event then you must produce a brief describing the parameters of the event to everyone involved. Effective briefing is one of the most important parts of the organiser's job. In fact, it's perhaps the most important part of the event planning process. A clear, concise brief that's been well thought out and that doesn't need to change as the event begins to take shape is a blessing to all concerned, not least to the producer.

So what makes a good brief? It must make clear the event's objectives and list the resources that can be made available to achieve them. Whether it's spoken or written, the brief is meant to provoke a response, to generate ideas; so the organiser must prepare the brief so that everyone knows the parameters within which those ideas must work.

Preparing such a brief is a great way to clarify the mind. Even if the organiser is writing and producing the event alone it's a task that should still be performed, to be quite sure that the answers to questions such as the following are known.

DRAWING UP THE BRIEF

- *What type of event is being planned?*

- *When is the event to be held?*

- *Where is it to be held?*

- *Who is to be the target audience?*

- *What is the event's objective?*

- *Who or what is to be the 'star' of the event?*

- *What human resources can be made available?*

- *What technical resources?*

- *What is the budget?*

- *Who is to produce the event?*

Answers to these questions will provide the basic information for a brief. It's not strictly necessary to go further – for example, to spell out a concept the organiser has in mind. The organiser may have very specific ideas on the shape the event ought to take and good reasons for them, but it's usually best to give the bare bones of the brief and then wait for reactions, either from the in-house team or from outside specialists. Discussion of the concept can then take place at a later date without anyone feeling that irrevocable creative decisions have been made.

Incidentally, if you're using outside specialists beware of briefing too many different companies. Rightly or wrongly, clients doing this have gained a reputation for using the brief simply to extract ideas from production houses competing for the work; there's no real intention to award contracts. By the time the concept is being considered, however, the organiser will most probably have decided on a short-list of possible outside suppliers so no more than two or three competing companies should be involved.

THE CONCEPT

'Concept' is a word much bandied about by creative people, particularly when they've just been given a vague, meandering brief by an uncertain client. In those circumstances 'concept' comes to mean a suit of clothes with which to disguise the nakedness of the client's message. Depending on the creative team involved, the client may then be presented either with an immaculately tailored outfit so even if he's not sure how he feels, at least he'll look good; or he may be given some form of fancy dress and be expected to play a major role in a frenzied showbiz spectacular, despite the fact that he and his colleagues are soberly serious chartered accountants.

But change the word 'concept' to 'idea' and things become much simpler. Every event should start with an idea, and one of the organiser's most important jobs is to identify the idea behind the event and to keep it firmly in focus throughout the subsequent planning and production processes.

Finding the idea

So, how does a conference organiser find the idea that lifts the event out of the ordinary, and makes it effective and memorable? First of all the event needs to be analysed.

● *Why is it being held?*

There has to be a reason why your company intends to spend time and money on holding an event. Is it because the salesforce need to be given new targets, office staff informed of changes, the public persuaded to buy a new product or service, shareholders kept in the picture?

● *Who is the target audience – and what messages should they be receiving?*

Who is going to be invited to the event? Who is likely to be attending? Try to discover whether your intended audience has a generic character. What's their average age? Are they mostly men or women? What are they expecting from the event, what are you going to tell them – and do these two things coincide?

● *Who or what should be the 'star' of the event?*

The 'star' is the centrepiece of the event, its *raison d'être*, the theme around which everything revolves. It could be the new product you're launching; the important announcement the MD has to make; the unveiling of last year's results – good or bad; it might even be a real star, a personality whose job is to give some character and life to an event which has little or none of its own.

● *What is the size of the budget?*

It is not absolutely essential to know the precise amount, but it'll be necessary to have some idea of whether the budget is large, small or – as is usual – somewhere in between if you're to plan the event satisfactorily. It's sometimes difficult to prise budget details out of clients; 'You tell us what you intend to do and how much it will cost and we'll tell you whether we've got the budget to do it,' some say. If you can, refuse to play this game; it can go on for weeks with the producer rewriting outlines and formats time and again in order to match the client's ever-decreasing budget. Most clients have a fairly clear idea of the sort of money they're prepared to pay for their event and it's in their interest to tell you the sum they have in mind at the outset. If they refuse, suspect the worst and plan for the lowest of low-budget events.

● *Is there a preferred location for the event?*
If delegates are coming from all over the UK you'll probably be looking for a venue somewhere in the Midlands. Is it important to provide leisure activities at the location for delegates and/or their partners? If so, you may need to go out into the country to find the ideal venue. Are many people expected to bring their cars? If they are you might want to find somewhere either out of town or with excellent parking facilities.

Questions like these should be put at the very earliest stage of planning – and put very clearly too, for plain answers to them will lay a firm foundation for the event.

For example, if you ask a client why he wants to stage an event and he tells you he's planning to launch a new product, you'll know he's almost certainly expecting a colourful production carried out with a great deal of panache; on the other hand, a client representing a group of doctors or lawyers planning a convention would probably want a more serious approach; too much glamour and theatricality might be regarded as unprofessional and even possibly in bad taste.

The audience

Who is the target audience? It's an impossible question to answer, of course. An audience is made up of many different people, all with their own individual tastes, so unless you're very lucky you won't get a unanimous response from every one of them. You won't even get identical responses from different audiences, as anyone who has ever stayed in a cinema and watched a film through a second time with a different audience will tell you. But even though your researches can never be complete, it's vitally important to find out as much as you can about your potential audience.

Here is a good opening question that is less daft than it might sound: 'Do they all speak English?' I once found myself half-way through a briefing meeting when the client casually mentioned that the audience for his event would include several very important Japanese executives of the company, all of whom were gamely struggling with the English language. When it became evident that one of the client's major objectives was to impress these gentlemen the event began to take shape – with a far less aggressively British theme than the one we'd tentatively been planning.

With events being held internally – sales conferences, annual reviews, financial and strategic planning conferences, and so on – the 'in-house' organiser will often know many of the speakers and members of the audience personally, or at least will be able to obtain information on them easily enough. This can be a tremendous advantage. Knowledge of the strengths and weaknesses of speakers will help the organiser structure the event around the strongest elements, while an in-house audience will have its own culture which the organiser will do well to recognise if the aim is to impart credibility to the event.

A star is born

Having discovered the nature and composition of the audience, the organiser must now decide on the main feature of the event, its 'star' if you like. This 'star' may be a product, it may be a person or personality (they're not the same, as anyone who's worked with both will tell you) or it may be an idea – a changed way of working, perhaps, or a new approach to a market. There's usually only room for one star if the event is to achieve its objective, so it's important to make quite sure that both the organiser and the client – if they're different people – agree on its identity. Uncertainty about who or what is the real star of the show could lead, for example, to your expensively produced product launch being totally upstaged by a hired 'showbusiness' presenter whose personality overwhelms the messages you want to transmit.

Just ask yourself: who or what should the audience remember in the days and weeks following this event? The answer is the 'star' – and everything and everyone connected with the event must ensure that the star gets top billing, the best lines and the most memorable moments. But don't confuse entertainment with effectiveness. Rather like those terribly clever advertisements that make you laugh, although you can't quite remember the product, it's not enough simply to give your audience a good time; if the organiser is doing the job properly, they're having a good time because they are relaxed – in the right frame of mind to accept the messages they are being given.

So, having fixed the reason for the event, the likely composition of its audience and the identity of its 'star', all that remains is to come up with an idea to make it memorable.

IDEAS – AND HOW TO GET THEM

Where do good ideas come from? One engaging theory is that the hypothalamus produces most of the everyday 'good ideas' we have. For those of us not too hot on elementary neurosurgery, the hypothalamus is a chunk of brain somewhere around the back of the head which, if left to itself, is supposed to be capable of processing all our experience, knowledge and ability, and transmuting the whole crazy mess into a series of sparkling, newly-minted ideas. If this theory is true then perhaps the key phrase is '. . . if left to itself . . .'; for in this writer's experience good ideas rarely come from prolonged, painful, solitary sessions spent staring at a blank sheet of paper while thinking furiously.

If the ground work has been done, the organiser will know why the event's being held, who'll be in the audience and what messages they need to receive. In other words, in the organiser's mind will be all the ingredients which go to make up the event that's being planned. Leave to stand for a few hours (or better, days) and something – it may even be the hypothalamus – invariably goes to work to mix these ingredients with others already in the memory. And that's when an idea, perhaps even **THE** idea, will come. An alternative method is to get together with others in a 'brainstorming' session. A group of people bringing individual talents and experiences to bear on a common problem can often make a breakthrough and arrive at a fresh, new approach to an overfamiliar subject, while individuals might find it difficult to distance themselves sufficiently to make that conceptual leap. It's a matter of mentally 'standing back' from the problem, then confronting it from a completely different and untried angle. Here are just two examples.

A company had built up a strong reputation for the quality of its annual industry awards presentations. These were lavish, hi-tech affairs staged in some of the most modern venues around the UK. The client had decided that London was to be the next location, but as planning began it became apparent that all the suitable modern, technically well-equipped venues were already booked. The brief asked for 'a uniquely memorable event' and the decision was taken to change the character of the presentation radically. A City of London Livery Hall was booked, the oak-panelled, historic setting transformed into a seventeenth-century banqueting hall using imaginative lighting and the bare minimum of scenery, and an evening of Elizabethan entertainment devised which would complement the awards presentations. Not only did this approach work well, portraying the client's company as a somewhat warmer, more human organisation; it took place at the height of the recession and many in the audience were impressed by the company's adoption of a more economic presentation style. It also has to be said that in such an historic venue it would have been impossible to install a complex set; the trustees of the building frowned upon any suggestion that heavy lighting rigs might be suspended from their valuable ceiling, so the 'Elizabethan' idea of using just a few lights to simulate flickering firelight, some colourful banners and music of the period to set the scene, was not only successful but also a very economic solution to a venue problem.

A transport company about to launch a new service to France wanted to invite selected press representatives and a few potential UK customers to a launch event. The total audience size would be around thirty people. The client came clean right at the start: 'We haven't got any money for this,' he said. 'But it's got to be a really knock-out event showing everyone we really know about France!'

He was right about the budget – there was far too little even to think about taking the audience to France. So, instead, the production team began to think of ways to bring France to them.

After receiving invitations to an event which hinted at France as a possible location, audience members were picked up individually by cars provided by the transport company and driven to a small airfield in Surrey. There, they were ushered into a small building – a Nissen hut – as if to prepare for a flight to France. But once inside the hut they discovered their journey would be unnecessary for the interior had been created to resemble a tiny section of France. A Customs barrier had to be negotiated, then there were shops, a bistro, a bar, all very simply constructed but with insistent accordion music and the tang of Gauloises cigarettes in the background, all very realistic. A few native French speakers hired from local restaurants and hotels served good, simple French food, wine, coffee and croissants were freely available and it wasn't long before the audience was ready for the message. It was delivered via a twin projector audio-visual presentation which began as a gentle 'send-up' of a French *avant garde* film and developed into a programme powerfully demonstrating the transport company's knowledge of its French market.

The entire 'visit' to France lasted for around three hours, after which the guests were driven back to their offices bearing a few inexpensive but typically French gifts and an information kit containing a Michelin map of the areas served by the company – most useful on holiday trips.

Both these examples show there's no better stimulus for ideas than a shortage of money! Overinflated budgets often spawn vast, unwieldy events which simply consume facilities without making them work for their living. The next time you're stuck for an idea for an event, try halving the budget and see what happens!

But do you need an idea?

Is it really necessary to spend so much time and effort thinking of a way to present the event to its audience? The short answer is, yes, if you want it to work. Whether you're planning a businesslike, no-nonsense conference or a spectacular product launch, spending time on considering how the event will appear to its audience will be time well spent. Perhaps the best way to do this is to imagine you're a typical member of the audience and you're experiencing the event yourself. Does it surprise you, excite you, interest you, involve you? Was it worth attending? Are you learning something you didn't know before? Are you getting your money's worth? Organisers who want to improve their performance should be putting questions like these to the real audience after the event has actually taken place, but it's a very good idea to rehearse them beforehand and to 'hear' the responses. If you've done your homework on the nature of the audience and you can successfully identify with their attitudes and feelings as they metaphorically take their seats, if you're honest you may come up with some surprisingly critical comments. And it's better to be aware of those comments before the event rather than after.

Audiences for what we might call non-theatrical events – seminars, professional conferences, financial presentations and the like – are generally there to get right down to business so the organiser's overriding aim ought to be to devise a structure which is virtually invisible. The 'idea' of such events is to enable information to flow freely, so it's usually not advisable to confuse matters by dressing them up with too much character and theatricality. Everything must be subordinate to conveying information; if the event has any character at all, it should be one of simple, calm efficiency.

Do you need a *new* idea?

Events which benefit from a more theatrical approach – product launches, sales conferences, corporate presentations and so on – usually need an 'idea' to bring them to life – and the better the idea the more lively the event. The organiser struggling to come up with the great, sure fire, 100 per cent original idea, however, will perhaps be comforted by the news that it doesn't exist. Most of the scenarios and scripts written for theatrical presentations in the business world aren't wildly original and it's not terribly important that they should be.

Many very successful events have been structured around existing formats and characters 'borrowed' from television shows, films, plays and so on, and these have the great virtue that the audience knows what to expect. They're familiar with the plot line, the characters and the setting, so the event can get straight down to business. And even if an original, new approach is adopted, it's important to avoid extremes, to rule out any form of presentation that makes an impression in its own right. It's perfectly permissible to entertain the audience – in fact it's highly desirable if you want to gain and keep their attention – but never forget that they should remember your message, not the means by which you deliver it.

Who decides?

Despite my earlier comments concerning the tortuous nature of idea generation, you can be sure that once people know you're planning an event there'll be no shortage of sparkling new concepts coming at you from all directions. Everyone's a producer – until the moment it's discovered that boring things like budgets, administration, schedules and travel arrangements are all part of the job too, whereupon enthusiasm tends to wane.

Should you pay any attention to all these well-meaning contributions? Certainly. The most annoying thing about good ideas is that the most unlikely people can have them. People working inside your company, whether they're making policy decisions in the boardroom or tying up parcels in the mailroom, know what they'd like your event to say, so it's well worth sounding out as many different 'insiders' as you can to discover their thoughts – if they don't get to you first. You'll no doubt have to filter out the inevitable company gripes and pick your way diplomatically through a number of smouldering inter-departmental jealousies, but the exercise is generally worth the effort. You may even come across a really good idea once in a while, though you'll be lucky if it passes the three acid tests:

- Can we do it in time?

- Can we afford it?

- Will it get our message across?

If you've appointed an in-house production team, you stand a very good chance of coming up with a really good idea simply by sitting around and talking about it. The best ideas are those that simply . . . arrive. I can remember attending meetings which produced superb ideas, but I can't honestly claim sole credit for them and I doubt whether any of the company personnel also present would either. In those instances I perhaps performed a particularly useful function because I was an 'outsider' – I had no axe to grind on behalf of one department or another, my only intention was to help the companies concerned arrive at the best possible idea for their event. An outside agency or production house can often perform this function very well indeed, providing it has the ability to listen carefully to clients and to hear what they are trying to say to their audience.

If you're not using any outside help, then your in-house team is going to have to develop its own ideas without the benefit of an independent viewpoint. With obvious warnings about company gripes and inter-departmental jealousies, this can be achieved very successfully, particularly if the team has been selected to represent a wide cross-section of employees. They'll have a finger on the pulse of your company in a way an outsider can never have and, providing their efforts are moulded and guided sympathetically, they should come up with all the elements of the good idea you're after, even if you have to mould it into usable shape.

THE SECOND PRODUCTION MEETING

The first production meeting set out the terms of the event and briefed the production team on the logistical and creative requirements. The next stage is to choose the best idea or concept and to call a second production meeting to announce it to the production team and to commission the writing of a script.

Here's where the organiser who is also the producer begins to earn some keep, for in the conference world the decision to set the event on its irrevocable course by choosing this idea or that must be the organiser's alone, the first of many lone decisions that must be taken. A committee decision is just not possible; producing almost any kind of 'live' event requires many decisions to be made, some of them instantly, and a committee just couldn't react quickly enough. To use a naval analogy, the producer is like the captain of a ship; determining the course, issuing the orders and taking total responsibility for the success or failure of the venture. If a ship runs aground while the captain sleeps, naval law holds him to blame, even though he may have had no sleep for days beforehand. He cannot pass the blame on to subordinates. The producer, like the captain, is in sole charge of the event – and though the producer may wield power democratically, ultimate responsibility must not be shirked.

The wise producer recognises from the start that the help of talented people will be needed if the event is to be successful, so when the production team gathers to hear the producer reveal the theme, the idea, the concept that will carry the weight of the event, the producer will almost certainly structure the meeting as a discussion. Present at this meeting should be the designer, the writer, the production manager and a senior representative from the company commissioning the event; the agenda should be flexible; and the producer should do all that is possible to gain the confidence, the enthusiasm and the trust of colleagues, inviting their comments at all times.

A stage layout that may have been difficult for the organiser/producer to visualise can become plain when a designer describes it; technical details the producer may have forgotten the production manager will have to hand; the writer might suggest a slight change in structure to make the event more effective; and the company representative could contribute valuable technical or personal information to the discussion. It may sound too good to be true and in fact it is; many early production meetings are a bit of a shambles, with everyone trying to throw in ideas at the same time. But at most meetings ideas are being thrown in, and that's what counts.

At the end of the second production meeting, everyone should know in broad terms how the event is going to look to its audience and why it's going to look that way. Whether you call it the concept, the idea or the theme, it's the engine that will drive the event on to its conclusion, successful or otherwise. How fast or how well that engine performs now becomes the responsibility of the writer, whose task will be examined in Chapter 5.

4 Choosing the Venue

- Finding and booking a venue • Venue categories
- Layouts and capacities • Choosing the venue
- Conference centres • Hotels • Colleges and
universities • Unconventional venues
- The importance of location • Overseas venues

FINDING AND BOOKING A VENUE

The choice of a venue may be all-important – but it may also prove difficult or even impossible to select the ideal venue, simply because someone else has booked it first. There is a shortage of good conference venues in the UK and, although the opening of several fine new conference centres around the country has eased the problem a little, the great demand for high-quality conference space is still being met by too few locations.

The obvious moral is – get in first and book your conference venue well in advance. There is even a good argument for putting venue booking at the head of the 'Things to Do' list when planning an event, although strictly speaking the planning stages mentioned earlier should come first. The best advice of all, of course, is to begin the whole planning process well in advance; not only will the extra time spent planning and preparing be of benefit to the event, but there will almost certainly be a far better choice of available venues.

But the demand for good conference space is currently high and some companies are booking venues up to a year in advance – not a commitment every company wants to make. The question is: do you book a venue well in advance, risking a change in conference plans later on? Or do you leave venue booking until a few months or weeks before the event and risk its unavailability?

There is a third alternative. A number of good organisations specialising in venue selection and booking exist, and their help could be sought. In fact, considering the importance of the choice of venue and the difficulties often experienced not only in booking but also in selecting the right location for an event, it makes good sense to use a specialist in these matters.

For the company conference buyer, selecting a conference venue can be a time-consuming operation. Brochure-gathering is no problem – phone calls to the hotels, conference centres and local authorities in your target area will soon see to that. But checking out the brochure claims and making an honest assessment of the quality of service and facilities offered must involve personal visits. The specialist venue-finding and booking agency will have up-to-date information on a wide range of venues around the UK and abroad, provide excellent service, charge the conference organiser nothing (agencies receive commission from venues they 'place') and can not only advise on conventional venues and locations, but also suggest less conventional solutions to venue-finding problems. Incidentally, if you do use an agency it's important to give them time to do the job properly; they often complain that clients come to them after failing to find a suitable venue themselves, expecting the agency to succeed where they've failed, at very short notice.

If you frequently organise conferences it might be worth considering membership of the Association of Conference Executives (ACE International, address on page 201), which holds regular meetings for buyers and suppliers providing useful opportunities for the exchange of information.

VENUE CATEGORIES

Conference venues fall into three main categories: purpose-built conference centres; spaces offered by hotels in which conferences may be held; and college and university facilities.

Purpose-built centres can usually accommodate a large

number of delegates, offer facilities such as 'break-out' areas and catering services specifically designed to cater to the conference market, and are equipped to a fairly high technical standard. Access is generally good. Very limited overnight accommodation is sometimes offered within the centre, but this tends to be for VIPs only – a matter of four or five rooms perhaps. Delegate accommodation must be arranged at nearby hotels and in popular locations this may not always be easily available. Although often situated in city centre locations, parking for a large number of delegates' cars tends to be fairly easy.

Hotels, on the other hand, vary greatly in the size of conference space offered. In some hotels arranging 'break-out' areas and catering services can call for a certain amount of ingenuity if the event is a large one; technical facilities are usually basic and not always to be trusted; access may be difficult and parking limited; but overnight accommodation is usually available, and standards of food and service can be high in the better hotels.

Colleges and universities offer their facilities in out-of-term periods only, which can be restrictive. But highly competitive rates, accommodation allowing delegates to live 'on-site' for the duration of the event and the provision of purpose-built lecture halls are advantages. The standard of accommodation and catering can be rather basic, however, making these venues more suitable for the more 'serious' events such as seminars, symposia and training.

LAYOUTS AND CAPACITIES

Although most venues will provide a guide to room capacities, the number of people who comfortably fit into a room will vary depending upon the type of layout the event demands. The number of different layouts available is infinite, but according to some authorities the three most commonly-used are classroom, with desks and seats ranged in rows; theatre, where the seat rows are closer together and no desk space is provided; and reception, where perhaps only a few or no seats are provided. The table opposite gives a guide to the approximate capacities of areas using these layouts.

Number of people	Area in square metres needed for layouts		
	Classroom	Theatre	Reception
10	16	*	*
15	24	*	*
20	32	15	*
25	40	19	*
30	48	23	18
40	64	30	24
50	80	38	30
75	120	57	45
100	200	75	60
125	230	93	75
150	**	112	85
200	**	150	115
300	**	230***	175
400	**	300***	235
500	**	400***	300
1000	**	745***	600
1500	**	1120***	900
2000	**	1500***	

*   Allow plenty of space even though numbers are small
** Tiered lecture theatres or theatre layout recommended
*** Theatre with fixed seating recommended

(Note: Large sets or bulky presentation equipment can reduce the above capacities.)

Another useful method of categorising layouts and calculating their capacities has been devised by BACT (British Association of Conference Towns). This is shown overleaf.

As a guide to the capacities of these different layouts, a room that can accommodate 100 people theatre style can normally be used to hold:

● twenty-five people in boardroom or U-shape

● fifty people in school/classroom

VENUE LAYOUTS

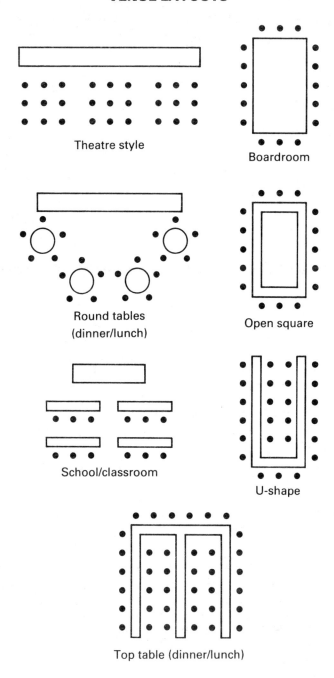

Theatre style

Boardroom

Round tables
(dinner/lunch)

Open square

School/classroom

U-shape

Top table (dinner/lunch)

- fifty people in theatre style with lunch

- seventy-five people in round tables/top table.

CHOOSING THE VENUE

So, with a pile of glossy brochures describing a multitude of 'ideal' venues in front of you, how do you, the conference organiser, choose the one you know will be perfect for your event?

First, or course, you should know what you're looking for in terms of location, meeting-room size, and quantity and quality of accommodation, as well as the quality of food and service you think appropriate to the delegates attending the event.

A survey carried out by the QE2 Conference Centre in London revealed that the vast majority of conference buyers considered a high standard of service the most important factor in selecting a conference venue. Then, in descending order of desirability, they wanted an experienced senior person from the venue assigned to the event; a purpose-built conference room; and a high standard of security. Undoubtedly, factors such as location, room size and price also had parts to play in the selection process, but it's interesting to note that three out of the first four factors mentioned are concerned with service.

Once you've found a space that you think is in the right place, has the right shape and quality and is big enough for your event, stand in it for a few moments and ask yourself some questions. A checklist is provided on the following page.

And, before you go, take a seat in the empty room, imagine the event is taking place, try to think of everything that could possibly go wrong – and devise a Plan B to handle it. Seasoned conference organisers will smile wryly at this point; they know that however diligently this task is performed something unexpected almost always happens. But if you're to deal with it, it's vital to know the venue inside out, to know where everything is, what works and what doesn't, and whom you can rely upon in an emergency.

71

VENUE CHECKLIST

- *With the doors closed, is the room quiet?*

- *Are there pillars which might impede the delegates' view?*

- *If you need to, can you 'black out' the room easily?*

- *Is the ceiling high enough to hang lights if you need them?*

- *Would the walls or ceiling support heavy lights or a lighting grid?*

- *Are there enough electrical points? And where are they?*

- *Where are the lavatories – and are there enough of them to cope with all your delegates?*

- *Is there a cloakroom? If not, where do delegates' coats go?*

CONFERENCE CENTRES

For events designed to attract more than a few hundred delegates, the purpose-built conference centre is not only ideal, it is almost certainly the only possible choice. There are a growing number of such centres in the UK, some capable of holding audiences of up to 5,000, and for companies planning to hold a major event overseas there are many well-equipped and attractively-designed conference centres throughout Europe and the USA. Contacts able to give information on conference centres are listed on pages 178–203.

Conference centres offer technical sophistication, usually backed by knowledgeable support staff; access is easy both for delegates and sets – in many centres a double-decker bus can be brought on stage if required! – and most centres also offer smaller spaces which may either be used in conjunction with the main event, for exhibitions or 'break-out' areas, or for individual events involving smaller audiences.

But conference centres do not provide accommodation; this

must be arranged separately by the conference organiser. It is often possible to rely on the expert help of the conference centre staff, but when the centre is situated in a particularly attractive location – as many are – it's best to avoid peak holiday periods when there is a great demand for hotel space.

If the event you are planning is large enough to require the full complement of facilities offered by a major conference centre you will almost certainly be using a professional conference production company. When selecting such a venue, therefore, it is essential to consult with the chosen production company – although in practice the choice of venue is usually a joint decision made at an early planning stage. It had better be a very early planning stage however; conference centres are popular venues and are often booked months, even years, in advance.

HOTELS

In terms of specialised equipment and dedicated conference facilities most hotels trail some way behind purpose-built conference centres. But hotels can offer comfort, good food and service, factors which can more than compensate for their shortcomings in other respects. Hotels are also often chosen by organisers of the important small event sector where, although the number of delegates attending is far fewer – perhaps less than twenty-five – their company status is likely to be fairly high and this must be matched by the standards offered by the venue. With this in mind – and because hotels still represent by far the biggest slice of the conference venue market – it's worth examining the hotel sector in some detail.

There is, of course, only one way to discover whether the impeccable standard of service offered by an hotel really exists. You go there and try it. No matter how attractive the brochure, how efficient the conference manager sounds on the telephone, how promptly the hotel responds by letter, spend a little time there in person before you make your booking. Keep a low profile – in other words, don't tell anyone you're there to assess the hotel's suitability for your event – but do try to test some of the facilities you might need for it. Send an urgent fax; ask for secretarial services; leave some 'confidential' documents with reception to test security; meet the conference manager in person and ask to be shown the facilities the hotel offers.

These and any other tests you can usefully devise will not only be invaluable in helping to assess the true worth of the venue – they should also enable you to write a venue report. Compiling a number of these reports will provide a useful guide to the standards generally prevailing and it will also help the organiser build a precise specification of the facilities required for the event.

Here is a typical venue report based on an hotel situated somewhere in the south-west of England – names have been changed for obvious reasons!

THE BRIDGE HOTEL

A fairly typical hotel offering conference facilities. It's rated as a 3-star establishment, though at present it's realistically in the upper second for environment and service. The banqueting menus offered aren't all they might be; prices are uppish and the selection isn't wildly exciting. Better menus are available, but only for small groups (up to 35 covers).

As in many hotels, the conference manager (Tony O'Donoghue – pleasant and helpful) is a 'space booker' – he doesn't have a great deal of technical knowledge and couldn't be expected to play an important part in actually running a conference – he's there in a liaison capacity only. The grandly titled assistant conference manager is young and inexperienced, but willing and helpful. Good co-operation could be expected from them both.

Technical facilities are those typically offered by the better hotels: VHS/Beta/U-Matic VCRs and monitors; a slide projector with a screen; OHP and flip charts; microphones for the hotel PA system; and a 16mm sound projector with a choice of three screen sizes. Only the VHS machine was demonstrated; further checks on the other equipment would be necessary.

The hotel claims to offer 'a full range of secretarial services'. This appears to consist of the use of the hotel administration office with its staff of two, an IBM PC (WordPerfect 5.1), a new, fully-featured photocopier (A3, reduction, collation) and an old, well-used fax machine. I sent a fax (quick and efficient service), but no great reliance should be placed upon the ability of the secretarial staff to provide a full service when the hotel is busy.

The 'Anglesey Ballroom' is the largest space The Bridge Hotel offers. It's 26.23m × 15.25m × 5.49m high and capable of holding up to 450 conference delegates 'theatre' style, depending upon the set size. Double door access is good (2m × 3.50m wide). Last year a major car launch was held here and I was told it used 'a lot of big scenery'.

The 'Tower Ballroom' is on ground floor level and with a maximum door size of 2m × 2.28m wide, access for all but the very largest sets should be easy. The 'Tower' may be divided in two and there are five other suites suitable for conferences. In 'theatre' style these could hold betweeen 20 to 80 delegates.

There are 2 'VIP suites', 70 twin rooms and 35 single rooms. On a scale of ten, quality was rated at seven. Room service was good, cheerful and efficient. The two 'VIP suites' both offer good quality accommodation.

Parking's not easy around the hotel. The receptionist told me the hotel had underground space for 400 cars, but I later learned the figure was closer to 175. On-street parking is difficult close to the hotel. The nearest multi-storey car park is about half a mile away. The railway station (with plentiful taxis) is a mile and a half from the hotel.

I was assured that security is high – but every hotel says this. On the positive side, a notebook 'accidentally' left in the bar was returned to my room almost immediately; however, on my arrival at the Bridge Hotel I discovered it was possible to walk past reception and into any one of the conference rooms without identifying myself. If this hotel is used it will be necessary to keep an extremely close eye on the security measures adopted.

Although the Bridge Hotel space couldn't really be termed 'purpose-built' for conferences it has plenty of conference potential. Currently the hotel is selling its smaller spaces quite well, and there was a conference for 200 the week before this visit. When the car launch was mentioned, however, the comment was made that the hotel 'would like to host these big events more often'. Possibility of rate negotiation here perhaps? To date, most big conference bookings have been made almost exclusively through London agencies.

Incidentally, when checking hotel space don't forget to check on the size of access doors. One organiser overlooked this and found that before his impressive – and expensive – set could be taken into the conference room it first had to be sawn in half in the hotel car park!

The conference organiser reading the venue report given above should now start asking a few questions based on the information gathered.

ASSESSING THE VENUE

- Access isn't easy. Will delegates drive to the venue? Or will it be necessary to arrange trains and taxis? If many drive, car parking spaces should be booked at the hotel or arranged elsewhere.

- As the venue is in the south-west there is probably some attractive feature – countryside or coast – to make it worth considering. Are there also suitable leisure activities which could be arranged for delegates?

- Technical facilities at the venue are limited. Check availability of facilities and/or technical expertise locally, or be prepared to take whatever equipment and staff are needed.

- Security might need to be tightened. Check availability of local security personnel or be prepared to arrange own security cover.

- Is there a real possibility of price reductions at this venue? Make an enquiry!

COLLEGES AND UNIVERSITIES

Some colleges and universities offer excellent conference facilities, particularly for meetings of professional bodies or institutions where a more formal presentational style is appropriate. If you're looking for a purpose-built lecture hall with tiered seating and modern presentation equipment, one of the groups specialising in the out-of-term use of educational facilities may be able to help. Accommodation is usually available on site – typically the quality is adequate rather than luxurious – and although some modern universities seem to be located in rather remote areas, and all educational establishments suffer from the restriction that they can't be used in term time, they can offer an ideal combination of qualities to many conference planners. In fact, college and university facilities are so popular they are often booked well in advance; an early call to one of the specialist groups mentioned above is advised – addresses on pages 178–203.

UNCONVENTIONAL VENUES

The venue you choose can say a great deal about the message you wish your conference to convey. To take two simple examples: an impressive, dark-panelled meeting room in an Edwardian hotel could promote a certain seriousness and sense of occasion; an airy, modern white-painted room with lots of light flooding in through large windows might, on the other hand, generate an optimistic, no-holds-barred feeling among delegates. Similarly, the choice of a venue with an unusual character of its own can 'colour' the event in a way which could prove extremely useful to the conference organiser.

Conferences have been held on ships, aircraft, trains and even (in America, naturally) underwater, but there's no need to go to such extravagant lengths to achieve an effect. For example, a half-dozen or so top executives meeting to discuss strategy or make policy decisions might well find that instead of a luxurious, flagship hotel in the centre of London, a small, relatively modest but exquisitely-located country hotel could better provide the calm, relaxed atmosphere they need. Similarly, a venue that moves – a ship or a train – has an excitement of its own which can add a great deal to the impact of an event. You choose the venue to complement and perhaps reinforce the style and character of the event being planned – which is a very good reason for considering the choice of venue as early as possible in the planning process, just as soon as you have a firm idea of the shape and nature of the event.

Unusual venues may have a charm of their own, but they can also present unusual problems. Access to that exquisite country hotel or the old paddle steamer moored in some deserted creek may prove difficult and it's unrealistic to expect much in the way of modern communication facilities from such venues. Any venue that moves can present problems if you're thinking of using slides or video to any great extent; a sales conference on a train ran into trouble when its beautifully produced audio-visual programme lost much of its smooth, unhurried quality as the carriages rattled noisily over points and other trains roared past in the opposite direction. And there's the – possibly apocryphal – story of 100 car dealers and their motor manufacturer hosts marooned on a broken-down cruise ship in an increasingly hostile Irish Sea.

But such tales of woe shouldn't prevent you from exploring the possibility of using somewhere different for your event. The transport company that took its key staff off to the races, then gave them a presentation on the theme of 'Quality Thoroughbreds' in an on-course hospitality suite had a hit on its hands; and so did the food manufacturing organisation that dispatched its marketing managers to a Scottish castle where, after a busy day spent examining the market potential of a new product, the big event of the evening was a grand feast, complete with pipers and featuring the product itself. A venue with a character of its own can almost write your event for you.

THE IMPORTANCE OF LOCATION

The choice of a venue is often dictated by its location; unfortunately, this often means that many conference organisers settle for a second-best venue that is nearby rather than risk the cost and uncertainty of shipping delegates to a perfect venue that happens to be a few hours away. It's an understandable trade-off, but it can jeopardise the chances of a successful event.

The character and quality of the venue are extremely important. Rather than choosing a second-rate venue that is conveniently just around the corner, it is often the case that choosing the right venue in the 'wrong' place can bring powerful benefits. First, delegates may welcome a chance to meet in a fresh, new location; and second, the mere act of travelling can not only be a powerful 'scene-setter', it can also be planned to form an integral part of the conference itself.

In the UK, for example, 150 executives boarded a specially-booked conference train at Paddington for a journey to a west-country seaside resort hotel where a sales conference was to be held.

During the three-hour trip the executives were given a presentation announcing an incentive scheme, formed a number of teams to take part in a quiz competition and were awarded prizes for the successful completion of a questionnaire. By the time they arrived at their west-country destination they were, in the words of the company's conference organiser, 'primed and ready to go'. Far from being a disadvantage, the three-hour journey offered an ideal opportunity to get delegates in the conference mood.

OVERSEAS VENUES

Despite a growing number of high-quality conference venues in the UK there can be very good reasons to take delegates to a venue abroad. Overseas travel can add a flavour of excitement to an event, delegates may feel stimulated by the sights and sounds of a foreign country – and as most overseas conference organisers tend to head for the sun everyone usually enjoys the weather.

Perhaps surprisingly, cost-saving can be a deciding factor too. If a truly international event is being planned with delegates coming from a number of different countries, it can make economic sense to stage it in a country which the majority of delegates can reach easily and fairly inexpensively. Many overseas events feature an incentive element and this too can justify the choice of an exotic or unusual foreign location, particularly if a well-planned and productive working programme can be incorporated into the event.

There's not a great deal of difference between organising a conference in Manchester or Monaco. You'll still have to visit the venue, ask the right questions about it and test the claims it makes (see page 76), although it's sometimes possible for the travel costs of this operation to be met by the venue owners or operators.

Getting there

But although choosing the venue and organising an overseas event may be as easy – or as difficult – as a home-based event, organising overseas travel arrangements for perhaps hundreds of delegates can be an administrative nightmare. It is not simply a matter of booking the right airline tickets – although that can provide enough pitfalls; there are transfers to and from the airport to be organised, couriers and translators to be arranged, sightseeing tours and recreational facilities booked – the list can be endless. Unless you have had a great deal of previous experience in these matters, you would be well advised to hand over all the travel and overseas arrangements to a specialist travel agent.

Note the word 'specialist'. Some otherwise perfectly efficient local travel agents often claim to be able to handle this kind of work; but it demands such a detailed knowledge of the resources available in the host country – not to mention the conditions and laws covering their use – it's far better to appoint an agency which has had experience in the country concerned and knows how to keep your event running smoothly. A list of overseas travel agents specialising in group and conference travel can be obtained from one of the trade organisations listed on pages 201–203 at the end of this book.

5 WRITING A CONFERENCE

- Choosing a writer • Writing for speech • Some guidelines for speechwriting • The brief • The script

CHOOSING A WRITER

Everyone's a writer. Or, to put it another way, everyone can write. But the person who turns out witty reports or entertaining memos may not necessarily be capable of the sustained and skilful effort involved in writing a conference script.

Of course, some conference events don't need scripts at all. For example, a group of managers meeting to discuss company policy probably won't be speaking from detailed scripts; a good agenda will let everyone know when they're expected to speak and, as specialists in their own disciplines, they'll know precisely what they want to say.

But the majority of events do need writing, or at least constructing on paper, well before the day of the 'performance' arrives; for the script provides not just the words people say, but also a blueprint for the entire event, letting the designer know what kind of set will be required, giving the technicians information on the sound and light systems they'll be installing, and generally letting everyone have the opportunity to check that all the myriad 'bits and pieces' of an event are in place.

The script, in other words, can be regarded not so much as a work of art as a logistical checklist embroidered with a few well-chosen words. It's also, in its earliest form, very much a basis for negotiation rather than a tablet set in stone. Whoever tackles the job of producing a script, therefore, whether it's someone from inside your company or an outside specialist, should remember that conferences are produced by teams of people and the writer is just one member of a team. The writer's words can contribute a great deal to the success (or failure) of an event, but it's the writer's knowledge of conference staging and technicalities, his ability to work harmoniously with other members of the team and above all his flexibility which are the most valuable qualities a writer can bring to the job of producing a conference.

The freelance writer

Conference organisers who employ either a specialist production house or an outside producer may not have the opportunity to choose the person who is to write their event. This isn't greatly important; in both instances the writer is likely to be an experienced freelance who has a track record with the production house or producer concerned and will usually have been selected because he or she has written successful scripts for events similiar to the one about to be created.

Violent disagreements between freelance writers and clients are rare, possibly because they need each other but more likely because freelance writers are quite often surprisingly skilled in diplomacy; perhaps it's their persistent need to gather information that makes them so tactful! However, if you, as the client, find it difficult to work with a writer who doesn't seem to see the project your way then you have a serious problem.

The sensible thing to do is to have a discussion with your writer and other members of the production team to try to find some way of resolving the situation. But in the end, if it isn't possible for the writer to agree with the client's view of the project there can be no alternative but to find someone else. The chances of this occurring are remote – freelance producers are very selective about the writers they use and usually match writers to clients very effectively – but the writer must see things the client's way or the project is heading for disaster. This doesn't mean the writer has slavishly to agree with everything the client says; there'd be no fun in that for anyone. But it does mean the writer must be in broad agreement with the client's view of the project. If not, the writer must say so, must suggest a better alternative and, if the client isn't persuaded, then the writer must bow out as gracefully as possible.

The in-house writer

Working with an in-house writer, someone employed by your own company or organisation, can offer many advantages. Much tedious research can be avoided because the writer will probably know a great deal of the necessary background information; the characters and personalities who'll be involved in the event should be familiar; and lines of communication between the writer and the production team should be extremely short – indeed, they may all be working in the same building or office.

That's the good news. The not so good news is that even though your writer is an employee you'll still have to pay for the script. Researching and writing takes time – allow at least an hour for every minute of event running time for the writing alone – so whoever does the job will still be drawing a salary even though they are not doing their usual work. Presumably someone else will have to provide cover – and so on down the line, meaning that at some stage you'll almost certainly be facing extra expense or risking a loss of efficiency.

There are other possible drawbacks in employing an in-house writer. Such a person may not be fully aware of the technicalities involved in staging an event; his or her approach may be too insular – an outsider can often view a company's event with a fresher eye; and there can sometimes be problems with internal politics. If, for example, someone from sales is selected to write the event, employees from every other department will be noisily convinced they're inadequately represented.

What to look for in a writer

But let's suppose you've surmounted all these hurdles and finally arrived at the moment of decision: who is going to write your event? Given several candidates, all of whom are eager to do the job, have a fairly good appreciation of the technical aspects involved and are well-enough liked to extract relevant information from people at all levels in the company, whom should you choose?

If you discover a great dramatic writer who, for some years, has been hiding her light under your company's bushel, praise her to the skies and find a kind way to say you'll let her know. Similarly, the funny man in accounts who everyone thinks ought to be writing TV sitcoms should be encouraged to do so, but kept well away from your event. The writer you choose should be able to demonstrate two major qualities; a clear, logical mind and an ear for the way people speak.

As I said earlier, a conference script isn't meant to be a work of art, a piece of writing that has a life of its own. The script has to do a job, to deliver a message, and any kind of 'fine writing' would simply get in the way and obscure that message. So clarity of thought and expression is the ideal to aim at, rather than flowery phrases and clever verbal tricks. But make no mistake – writing simply and clearly is a great deal harder than it looks – or rather, sounds.

At a rehearsal for a large UK conference a while ago I was asked to comment on speeches various managers had written for themselves. One manager, in particular, was wondering what had gone wrong with the piece he'd so carefully written – and which was proving to be too difficult to deliver. It was all to do with increased sales in his area – or at least that's what everyone guessed it might be about. 'With regard to the marketing of processed milk products in Area Three,' he announced to a somewhat restless audience, 'the percentile increment in revenue appreciation in year on year terms demonstrated considerable growth throughout accounting period six.' I stopped him there and asked him to explain. 'Well, basically,' he said, 'we sold more yoghurt in East Anglia this year than we did last year.' I gently suggested it would be better to use simpler language to help those in the audience less familiar with company jargon. He gratefully agreed, seized a pen and started to amend his copy of the script. And as soon as he tried to put on to paper the words he'd just said, he felt the need to elaborate, to dress up the simple, clear statement 'We sold more yoghurt in East Anglia this year than we did last year' with longer words, technical words, specialist words – because WRITING words on to paper is often perceived to be far more important, more prestigious, than SPEAKING them out loud.

WRITING FOR SPEECH

I wrote at the beginning of this chapter 'Everyone's a writer', though perhaps I should have added 'And everyone's a speaker'. We all find it quite natural to process our thoughts into speech almost instantaneously and most of us do it quite well; surely it can't be too difficult to take those spoken words and pin them down on to paper? Fine in theory, but there is a saying – 'Thoughts fly, words go on foot' – which explains why writing words that sound natural when they're spoken is not an easy matter. If you can pin down a thought or a series of thoughts on paper in such a way that when they're spoken out loud they sound perfectly natural, you have either been practising hard for many years or you're a natural writer, someone who's blissfully, gloriously unaware of the difference between writing and speaking.

But perhaps the real secret of writing for speech is to listen to people speaking. The inflexions and rhythms of voices are fascinating, and I don't just mean accents; listen carefully to some voices and it's not only possible to hear where the owner came from, but also what sort of person they have become. Kind, angry, sad, joyous – it's usually all there in the voice and even if the speaker's uttering words in a dull, monotonous drone, that too is a guide to the speaker's character.

SOME GUIDELINES FOR SPEECHWRITING

Are there any rules for speechwriting? Not rules, perhaps, because every speaker will need a different treatment; but there are some guidelines which might help if you're faced with a terrifyingly blank sheet of paper upon which you must write down words someone else will have to speak.

● *Voices are instruments*

If you are writing for speech you should think of voices as instruments and yourself as a kind of musician. Make your words match the voice you're writing for – don't write piccolo words for a trombone player and vice versa.

● *Meet the voices*

It's very important to meet the speakers who will be taking part in the event. A face-to-face meeting is best because then you can see the speaker's features and body language – with some people as much a part of speech as the spoken word; but if all else fails telephone the speaker and listen to him talk.

● *Speak the words*

As you write, try out the words yourself; speak them out loud and try to judge how they'll sound to an audience. Ignore worried looks from your office colleagues, your partner or the neighbours; speech is meant to be heard and you'll never know what it sounds like until you try it. My filing cabinet has heard some awful speeches in its time, but they soon improved when I heard how bad they were!

● *Keep them simple*

There are some words that look fine on paper, but aren't all that easy to say. For example, 'innovative' is a good word for the corporate brochure but not necessarily for the corporate speech. If you're using unusual or difficult words, try to check that your speaker is happy with them. Better still, try to avoid them, along with all forms of slapdash corporate gobbledegook. If I hear another grey-suited figure rattling on about 'initiating a goal-oriented synergistic approach to corporate growth' I shall scream! There's nothing wrong with plain words so use 'try' instead of 'endeavour', 'buy' instead of 'purchase', 'about' instead of 'approximately', 'ask' instead of 'enquire' and so on.

● *Write 'signposts'*

Write your speech in sections with clear divisions between subjects so the speaker can navigate from one to another. These sections can be introduced by words or phrases which stand out from the preceding text – a change of gear signalling the start of a new theme as it were.

● *Make the changes*
Don't ever think of the script you've written as something engraved in stone, never to be changed. However carefully you've done your homework there are going to be words and phrases in your script the speaker will find uncomfortable to say. Be ready to change them in a way that's helpful to the speaker, but that keeps the shape and sense of the speech as a whole.

So, to get back to your choice of writer, ideally you'll choose someone who can express himself on paper clearly and simply. Don't worry if your choice doesn't have a degree, comes from the wrong department and is outranked by everyone else on the production team; if he or she can take the raw materials of your event – the messages speakers want to deliver – and turn them into lively, informative and above all *interesting* speech, then your event is off to a flying start.

You'll probably have a good idea whom you'll choose to write your script, but if there's any doubt in your mind organise a test; pick some particularly dull subject – 'The Marketing of Processed Milk Products in Area Three', for example – and ask your shortlisted candidates to write a few minutes' worth of script, which *someone else* should then deliver. When you find yourself really listening to the presenter who sounds lively and interesting – then you've found your writer. And having found your writer, you must brief him.

THE BRIEF

Give the writer brochures, arrange for him to meet some or all of the participants in your event, make sure he is well and truly soaked in the traditions and character of your company – and tell him everything, up to and including the weaknesses of some of your speakers and the budget you intend to spend. If you have already decided on a theme for the event or have very definite ideas about how it ought to go, now is the time to tell the writer. He may not be able to see the event the way you do and you must give him the chance to say so. Clearly identify the person who has creative control of the event – and therefore who will make the final creative judgement on the script when it's written. Writers always want to know whom they've got to impress. And if you're a wise organiser or producer you'll ask them to develop their own ideas rather than follow a successful but well-trodden path. There's nothing more dispiriting for them than to discover they've been hired to fill in the blanks of some preordained script, an exercise in writing by numbers. Writers don't just write words, they have ideas too and they can be very good ideas.

And, having given every bit of background material you can think of, you must then ask your writer to exercise restraint and instead of diving headlong into a fully-fledged script, write an outline instead.

The outline

Like every operation connected with the organising of a conference, writing a script is best undertaken step by step, with an outline almost invariably coming first. Beware the organiser who suddenly cries 'I've got this great idea – let's get someone to write a script!' By all means ask someone to write a script around a carefully constructed outline, but if the ground work hasn't been done and the outline doesn't take into account the realities of the project, then it's very likely the script won't be much use. If the event's very simple or it's been done in the same location many times before perhaps you might skip the outline stage. Otherwise – don't.

What is an outline?

The outline is the skeleton upon which the event will be grown. If the bones don't join properly or the outline writer has tied a couple of sections together with a bit of verbal string just to make the thing stand up then it will quite possibly develop all sorts of horrific ailments as the production process continues.

Conversely, get the outline right and writing the script

becomes a much easier operation. The writer will not only know where the event is going, but also why it's going in a particular direction and what the script can do to help it reach its destination. And, just as important, the outline will allow everyone in the production team to have first sight of the project, and to contribute ideas and suggestions which may improve it.

If the event is fairly uncomplicated or it's been done many times before in the same location a detailed outline may not be necessary, although it's always a good idea to get down on paper a summary of aims and objectives, and a brief description of how the event will achieve them. It need only be a page or so, but it can provide a useful *aide-mémoire* for the producer should complications arise, as well as giving the production team a clear guide to the nature and shape of the event they're about to build.

On the other hand, if the event is breaking new ground – if it's the first production for the producer or for a new client; if it's being produced using unfamiliar facilities or locations; or if it's being constructed around people with whom the producer has not previously worked – then an outline is not only advisable but necessary. It's possible to avoid a great deal of trouble later on in the production process by using the outline as a way to think through every aspect of the event in advance and on paper.

Here are some of the headings frequently used to develop outlines. You don't have to use all these headings and you don't need to give them the names given here. But to illustrate the ground an outline can usefully cover, beside each heading is an idea of the type of information which may be included.

INTRODUCTION/BACKGROUND – A brief description of the projected event, why it is being held, why this outline is being written and what it is to contain.

OVERVIEW – Relevant information concerning the event. This might include information on the company and its market, a survey of previous events held by the company and any special considerations which the writer feels may need to be taken into account during the production process.

THE BRIEF – If a written brief has been received from the client, this should be played back to him, word for word, if it isn't too long, and with any additions or amendments suggested by the writer clearly marked. If only a verbal brief was received the writer should attempt to put down a clear recollection of what was said rather than his interpretation of it.

It is vitally important that the brief is understood to mean the same thing to both the company commissioning the event and the organiser or producer responsible for its production.

Misunderstandings about what the brief says and what it really means can – and do – cause a great many problems once the initial euphoric pre-production stage is passed and work begins on the details of the production. It's amost inevitable for there to be disagreements on some of these details later on, but it's essential that right at the beginning of the production process the producer is seen to agree with the client's broad intentions given in the brief. The outline gives the producer the opportunity of putting that agreement in writing, along with any reservations.

OBJECTIVES – The objectives the event is aiming to achieve should be described in the client's brief and once again it's a good idea to play them back to the client in the outline to make sure everyone agrees on them. By changing some details it's possible the event may be able to achieve objectives the client hadn't considered and here's where to describe what these additional objectives might be and what changes would be necessary to achieve them. The client may or may not be willing to make the changes but at least he will know that the outline writer is on his side and as eager to make the event a success.

VENUE AND DATES – Here the writer should either name the chosen venue with a brief indication of its facilities, size and availability; or list a number of suitable venues available for the specified dates of the event.

KEY CONSIDERATIONS – Anything which might materially affect the shape, cost or effectiveness of the production should be detailed and discussed here. For example, costs may increase if it's considered essential to hold the event in a certain place at a certain time; the presence of important guests could affect the creative approach; the client may want to repeat parts of the event elsewhere; alternatives suggested by the client or the producer may affect the budget. It's best to address these 'What if?' questions at an early stage and the outline is a good place to do it.

THEME – If the event needs some creative input this is the moment the outline writer crosses the boundary between fact and fancy. Until now, the writer has been dealing with hard facts – the size of the event, its location, the reasons for its creation and so on. Now, using all that information, some common sense and perhaps a little imagination the writer has to devise a theme which will make the event something more than just an ordinary meeting. There are no rules about this because there are so many variables; it depends upon the type of event being planned, the client's attitude, the composition of the audience and many other factors. Generally though, if enough thought has been given to the preceding parts of the outline the theme will often suggest itself.

CREATIVE TREATMENT – Based on the chosen theme, this is the heart of the outline, the part in which the writer takes the reader through the event from beginning to end in three or four pages. It's not a good idea to try to cover everything; it's fairly easy to write a twenty-page outline when there's so much detail to be described, but the really good outline, the one that catches a client's imagination, is the one that transmits the 'feel' of an event in just a couple of pages. One good way to do this – though by no means the only good way – is to write the piece from the point of view of a member of the audience. The creative treatment should give the client a good impression of what he will see and hear as the event takes place. If unusual equipment needs to be used or a special effect employed, the treatment may give brief technical details, but in general it should try to paint a picture of the event in fairly evocative terms – there's no need to go emotionally overboard, but the ability to write good, descriptive prose is very useful here. Well written, a tight, concise creative treatment can tell clients more about their forthcoming event than reams of analytical reports.

SOFTWARE AND HARDWARE SUPPORT – Not strictly speaking the writer's province, but very necessary in an outline not only to show that the writer is aware of technical matters but also to demonstrate the production team's ability to support the creative impetus of the project.

The time taken to research, prepare and write an outline might seem excessive; it's a document nobody performs, very few people see and one that has a very short lifespan. It isn't strictly speaking creative writing at all, more a semi-technical document examining the nuts and bolts of an event. But producing an outline is a vital first step in the production process. It gives the client the opportunity to 'see' the event for the first time and to understand why a particular approach has been adopted; it gives the production team a chance to anticipate the demands which may be made of them; and it allows the writer to be very certain of the reasons for adopting a creative approach and to try out on paper for the first time the ideas which may well develop into a script. If the outline is a good one, much of the time spent on it will be saved during the scripting stage, for a good outline puts down a firm foundation for the script – all the writer has to do is build on it.

The importance of the outline is widely underestimated. Many clients – and, it must be said, a good few production houses – regard an outline as a necessary evil, a document that has to be produced to gain the client's approval. Freelance writers are often paid poorly for outlines, but they do them in the hope they'll also be asked to write the much more lucrative script. It's the wrong way round; all the research, the thinking, the creative ideas go into the outline in compressed form. Once there, it's a fairly easy matter to decompress them and write the script – so the big money should really be paid for the outline, perhaps leaving the script to be dashed off by an apprentice. Well, it's a system that worked for that fellow who did the Sistine Chapel!

THE SCRIPT

The writer now heads for the trusty word processor and begins work on the first draft script. There will probably be three drafts; if the first draft sails through with very few or no amendments it's time to get very worried indeed – it usually means no one has read it properly and the big changes won't be demanded until a few days or even hours before the event.

All writers work differently so it's not possible to advise producers how to treat them while they're at work on the script. Support might be offered in the form of coffee or the occasional meal, but once you start asking 'How's it coming on then?', however sympathetic your tone you could be in for trouble. The best thing to do is lie low, say nothing – but be ready to answer any questions the writer may have as the script progresses. Here are a few typical examples of questions writers may ask.

● *How do I know how long my script runs?*
Depending on the content, a double-spaced A4 page generally runs about forty-five seconds to a minute.

● *Does script layout matter?*
No, so long as everyone can see a clear difference between descriptions of the set, technical instructions and speech. A very simple but effective layout is shown on page 95.

● *The MD doesn't want a script for his presentation – shall I write one anyway?*
No, but do a list of 'bullet points' which include all the subjects the MD intends to cover. Make sure the MD sees a copy of the script and agrees your list – and check that he or she is happy with the illustrations/slides/support material indicated in the script.

● *Mr X mumbles — how can I write his piece to help him speak more clearly?*

Leave a lot of space between the phrases. Try to use as many words as possible with open vowel sounds. Use every opportunity to make him look up – comments on slides etc.

● *Ms Y has given me far too much material – I've got to cut her drastically. How do I get around the problem?*

Go to her, explain your time constraints and ask for her help.

● *Mr Z still hasn't produced any material for me. How do I hurry him along?*

Ring him every day at the same time to remind him. Send him his script section – uncompleted. Send a copy of the running order with a big query against his name.

● *Miss W wants to see the whole script, not just her section. Should I give her a copy?*

Yes. Provided there are no security implications, she's right to want to know how her section fits into the event; but take no notice of amendments she makes to sections other than her own.

● *Our presenter is Mr A from sales – I think the event would be stronger with a professional presenter.*

That's the kind of discovery you can only make by writing a first draft script. The best solution is to write it for a professional. Then we'll either have to work wonders with the budget to afford the presenter we want, make major changes to the format – or find a way of turbocharging Mr A.

● *Mrs J is unhappy with my first draft. She wants to write her own piece. What should I do?*

Arrange a meeting with writer, producer and Mrs J. Explain impossibility of the DIY concept applied to conferences. Offer olive branch but insist writer must write Mrs J's piece.

● *The MD has changed his mind again and is now proposing a totally new format. Should writer begin work on this?*

Writer and producer check they have copies of outline MD agreed and signed. They take them to him. Explain impossibility of meeting target date if new format adopted now. If MD adamant, make judgement on whether to supervise disaster and resign later or resign now.

Of course, it's rarely as perilous as that last example might indicate, but as the script drafts start to appear tempers can

---

SAMPLE CONFERENCE SCRIPT LAYOUT

Production name and page no.

DIRECTIONS
THIS IS WHERE SET
DESCRIPTIONS AND STAGE
DIRECTIONS ARE GIVEN.
CAPITALS SHOULD BE USED AND
CLEAR DIVISIONS MADE BETWEEN
FACILITIES...

SOUND
A MUSIC CUE FOR EXAMPLE...

LIGHTS
OR A LIGHTING CHANGE.

SPEECH
The words delivered by speakers at
the event go here in normal upper
and lower case. If the technology's
available a second colour would be
useful.

◄——— (Leave a wide margin so everyone can make notes)

---

become a little frayed as the people who'll be speaking at the event see what the writer expects them to do. A wise writer will keep everything very simple, very straightforward. If there's some grand theatrical gesture the writer or producer wants to make they will keep it under their hat at this stage; the object of the exercise is to produce a script which everyone can agree, a script which will work technically and which delivers the intended messages. If the writer plans any extra twist to the production he would be well advised to wait until a few rehearsals have been held. If the production is progressing well then there may be an opportunity for something extra. But making the first draft script too ambitious is asking for trouble. Make it simple at first – add the tricks and clever bits only when rehearsals are going well.

And, finally, when at last you have a script everyone has agreed, make sure it's been signed by someone in authority. Changes will almost certainly be made as rehearsals progress, but that signed copy of the script is a safeguard preventing anyone from straying too far from the textual straight and narrow. Or it should do. In practice the speakers at the event must have the last word and no writer would argue with that. The speakers are the performers, the people who have the courage to stand and deliver in public; while writers mumble away to themselves or their filing cabinets as they perform alone, unable to face the tensions and uncertainties of the stage, failed actors every one!

6 CONFERENCE DESIGN

- What is design? • Briefing the designer • Print
- Signage • Reception areas • Exhibitions
- The set • Lighting • Design – in-house or buy in?

If your event is to go well and create the right impression on its audience it's important for it to look right; and 'looking right' doesn't simply mean that the drapes surrounding the Chief Executive's rostrum are the correct shade of royal purple.

How audiences react to an event depends on what they see as well as what they hear. The script may be a work of art, the speakers well rehearsed and confident, the venue perfect, but whatever kind of event it is, if it looks dowdy and dispiriting it's unlikely to do its job or satisfy its audiences. And if the design isn't right it can begin doing all these things long before the event itself begins.

So what is design, who is responsible for it and how can the conference organiser with little or no specialist design knowledge be sure his event is making the right visual impression?

WHAT IS DESIGN?

Design encompasses every visual element connected with an event; it can be identified as colour, shape or style; its effect begins as soon as members of your audience become aware of that event and should end only when the event has achieved its objective; and although good design will provide the best

97

possible environment for the event to succeed, bad design will almost certainly propel it rapidly towards failure.

What elements need design?

Design should be co-ordinated throughout an event; each visual element should complement and harmonise with every other. Signs used at the venue, for example, might echo the colours and typography used on the invitations. The need to produce a co-ordinated design scheme that will work effectively means that design must be considered at the earliest planning stages; ideally, the designer will contribute to the outline, working closely with the producer and writer to ensure that even at the very earliest stage design is integrated into the plan. Whether you're organising a straightforward seminar or a spectacular sales conference, design should be a consideration at every stage of the event – so let's start at the beginning and go through an event chronologically to see where design has a part to play.

BRIEFING THE DESIGNER

It's a very good idea to brief the designer and the writer together and at the same time. Ideally, the two should work together to create an outline which will combine words and images powerfully and effectively, and the two should also collaborate on the changes to the outline that may be necessary as well as on the script itself. In practice this rarely happens; designers and writers tend to meet only briefly – usually just before meeting the client to receive the brief – but usually they are both so aware that their meeting has to be as productive as possible that a great deal of communicating gets done in a very short time!

As a good organiser though, you will make it possible for designers to do their best work by following this checklist.

- Ensure the designer is there for the very first meeting.

- Consider the designer's ideas in tandem with those of the writer.

- Explain the event's objective clearly, paying particular attention to areas where design may have a strong contribution to make – a new image for a product or company, for example.

- Give a clear and accurate indication of the budget. For some reason the best designers always seem to think big; an advantage if the client has the imagination and courage to follow that lead, a disadvantage if the client's trying to stretch the budget as far as it'll go.

- Have the accurate dimensions of the venue and details of its technical facilities available. And in the case of larger events be prepared to pay for the designer to visit the venue, preferably in the company of the writer and any other key personnel.

- Allow the designer the opportunity to contribute to other activities connected with the event. These might include print, publicity, signage etc. Even if you are attempting to minimise costs by keeping some of these tasks in-house, there could be advantages in giving these responsibilities to an outside specialist so as to achieve the advantages of a totally co-ordinated design scheme.

PRINT

Long before the event takes place, the appearance of a printed invitation received in the post, an advertisement in a trade journal, even a simple note between departments within the same company inviting people to be present or to participate can establish the tone and quality of an event.

Print was once a commodity only experts could specify and order with certainty; printing techniques were often slow – and were slow to change – so print could also take a considerable time to produce. Now, with extremely high-quality printed images being delivered by laser and inkjet printers harnessed to computers running powerful desk-top publishing (DTP) software, the ability to produce good-looking print very quickly indeed can be found inside most offices. This chapter is concerned with design, however, so it must be said that although modern DTP software gives operators an astonishing ability to manipulate hundreds of different typefaces and a wide variety of images to help in the production of designs of every conceivable kind, it isn't clever enough to prevent the production of badly designed material.

Designing good-looking print is a skill few possess, but the enormous flexibility and resourcefulness of DTP software makes available to everyone most of the tools a skilled professional designer would use – except a designer's judgement. The software's been made as easy to use as possible so the temptation to dart from typeface to typeface, border to border, image to image is virtually irresistible, resulting very often in 'designs' that obey none of the rules of typography or layout and consequently look dreadful.

The problem is that everyone is aware of good print design, although it's usually a subliminal awareness. We're surrounded by expertly designed print; magazines, posters, advertisements, even the apparently haphazard layout of some tabloid newspapers – they've all been carefully and professionally created to attract us and persuade us to read the messages they contain. Design in these cases becomes virtually invisible; the typefaces used, their weights, colours and positioning mean nothing to the average reader. But the attractiveness of printed material and its readability depend upon the artful manipulation of these things; take away the professional layout and design skills, and you're left with a collection of unconnected marks that not only look unattractive, but also actively prevent your message being transmitted successfully.

The words you use to convey your printed message are, of course, important (and naturally they'll be correctly spelt – an otherwise well-designed brochure I recently received from a very prestigious company suffered terminally from the confusion between 'its' and 'it's'); but the design is the voice in which those words will be heard by the reader. Good design will make the voice smooth and persuasive; bad design can give your printed communications all the charm of a shifty street-corner lout.

If you're going to use in-house resources to design as well as print your own conference materials, the best advice is to keep the design simple. This is not the place to go into detail, but briefly it isn't a good idea to mix typeface families, ornaments should be avoided and 'design' should play a secondary role to readability. If your in-house print production team can get your message across cleanly and clearly they'll have been successful; asking them to create sophisticated design work might be asking for trouble, unless you have a professional designer or a talented amateur on the team.

SIGNAGE

As well as the signs used within the venue there is often a need to site signs outside the venue directing people to the building itself or to car parking spaces nearby. These, too, should follow your overall design scheme, remembering that members of the general public will also see them so their design and content could provide an opportunity to promote the name and image of your company.

If the event has a theme or a name this will probably be displayed at the entrance the venue. The conventional method is to hang banners on the façade of the building, although there are many variations on this theme. One company using 'Paths to Success' as the theme for a sales conference invited audience members to thread their way through a stylised maze as they approached the building, while another hired several magicians to mingle with the approaching audience performing sleight-of-hand tricks illustrating the 'Magic' theme chosen for the event.

RECEPTION AREAS

Inside the venue there are many more opportunities to 'brand' the event using design. At AGMs or similar events reception areas might use the colours or typography which identify the company or which link with the theme being used. Any stationery connected with the event – voter forms, registration documents and so on – should harmonise with the overall design scheme, and for events such as AGMs and similar corporate presentations where a company puts on a corporate face for members of the general public, it might be worth considering providing reception staff with uniforms complementing the event theme or reflecting the company image.

EXHIBITIONS

Exhibitions associated with AGMs or similar corporate events should be designed around the theme of the main event, using not only the visual elements of the theme but, wherever possible, its words as well. Exhibitions designed as an integral part of the event very effectively prepare an audience for what's to come, as well as helping to create a unified environment. Exhibitions or demonstrations held in conjunction with larger events are sometimes regarded as being separate, with the organisation delegated to someone outside the main production team. This is a mistake. From the moment an audience begins to interact with an event – which can be as soon as the invitation card arrives – to the moment the event is over and the audience leaves, it's essential that a unified image is presented with all the elements – including exhibitions and demonstrations – clearly seen as being part of a whole event rather than an assembly of separate units. Achieving this will be a great deal easier if one person is given total responsibility for the complete event, including the design content of any associated exhibitions or demonstrations. In some companies this may cause political problems; tradition might decree that responsibility for these activities always lies with a certain staff member or department. The only answer to this is to quote the 'captain of the ship' argument I've mentioned before; the event must leave a clear, unambiguous impression upon its audience and it's much more likely to do this if it's being controlled by one person with total responsibility for all aspects of the event. This isn't to say that the organiser or producer has to ride roughshod over the work of others who may know far more about their contribution to the event than he or she does; but for the audience to receive a coherent, co-ordinated message delivered through a unified design scheme, in my view it's necessary for one person to take full responsibility for all design aspects and that person must be the organiser or the producer.

However, it's nicer if the organiser or producer can be *given* full responsibility.

THE SET

Some events demand – and get – a set that wouldn't disgrace a West End stage. In fact, some product launch presentations have used stage facilities and techniques that leave the technical capabilities of the conventional theatre far behind. At the other end of the scale are events which need no set at all, at least not in the theatrical sense. Seminars, business conferences or training sessions perhaps don't need complex lighting rigs and specially made scenery, but it'll still be necessary to create environments in which delegates to these events can work comfortably.

The theatrical set

Designing and building a full-scale theatrical conference set is a job for professionals – a list of some of them appears on page 219. If you're using an outside production facility or freelance producer you can safely leave the choice and supervision of this resource to them, your only active involvement perhaps being to approve or comment upon the set 'mock-up' produced by the designer. This small-scale model will give everyone the opportunity to see precisely what the full-size set will look like and to anticipate any problems that may arise. Models produced for this purpose are often very finely detailed and can be quite costly, but at this stage the main features of the design have usually been agreed and it's unlikely that major revisions will be necessary. But the mock-up does give everyone involved a first sight of the set and an invaluable chance to visualise the event in action.

Some 'theatrical' examples
Theatrical conference sets vary greatly in size and complexity. The launch of a new motor car is often an occasion for superlatives and the set designer frequently follows suit.

A recent example held in a hall the size of an aircraft hangar featured an interior which had been designed to represent a

103

gigantic 'safety cell', surrounding the motor dealer dele gates with huge, reassuring structural shapes. When the presentation began, lighting effects cocooned the delegates inside this structure while video screens appeared magically from the darkness around them demonstrating the features of the new model in detail, but never showing the car in its entirety. This was saved for the 'product reveal' sequence, during which the car was lowered into the middle of the 'safety cell' on a glittering platform wreathed in clouds of dry ice, accompanied by suitably triumphant music. The manufacturer wanted to emphasise the strength and safety of the car to the dealer audience and design played a major part in this, with the 'cocooning' effect particularly being impressive.

At the other end of the scale, but equally effective for its purpose, a catering company with new organisation plans to reveal hired a fairly small hotel conference room and built a simple representation of a railway platform at one end, complete with booking office and waiting room. An actor, well-known for his comedy work, played the part of a station master and the entire event used a 'railway' analogy to convey to its staff audience the changes of direction and destination facing the company. The 'set' was kept simple, both for reasons of cost and portability; a painted backdrop was used to represent most of the 'platform' and the only construction necessary was the building of a small, free-standing hut representing the booking office and waiting room. Although perhaps a little 'joky' in character, this approach succeeded in conveying the required information in an entertaining way, with the responsibility for the effectiveness of the presentation mostly resting with the actor playing the station master's part; the set was simply a backdrop, inexpensive and easily erected.

The non-theatrical set

Although a set in the conventional sense isn't usually needed for seminars and similar events, some manipulation of the environment is often desirable or necessary and design has a role to play in this. For instance, a simple lectern artfully decorated with the event theme, a suitable company logo or even a swatch of velvet material can become a subtly commanding image, while even the differing height or size of chairs clustered around a seminar table can influence arguments and attitudes.

The function of design in these smaller, but no less important, events becomes not so much to impress as to enable. Clean, simple lines and clear colours can help to encourage alertness and participation, the seating layout should ensure that every delegate or audience member has an uninterrupted view of speakers, screens and blackboards, and lighting should play a major role in providing a comfortable, open environment for an event in which everyone can take part. The ability to design or construct a full-scale set isn't required here – just common sense and observation, and attention to detail.

Non-theatrical examples

Some of the most successful events I've seen were training sessions put together by a well-known chain store company. These took place in what had once been the ballroom of a large country house and they demonstrated the importance of audience layout. Comfortable chairs and small tables were dotted around apparently haphazardly, the general impression being one of completely relaxed informality. In fact, the layout had been carefully and craftily designed to encourage the maximum participation from every delegate – and it worked; in fact it was so successful tutors regularly reported difficulties in bringing sessions to an end – students were joining in so enthusiastically they didn't want to stop.

Also impressive were a number of day-long information sessions mounted by a financial company for its marketing people. These were held in a variety of venues around the UK and lacked any form of set. But in each very different venue the best possible use had been made of seating space and the technical aspects of the presentation went without a hitch every time. The company's marketing department had decided to base their presentation upon a number of self-contained slide-tape programmes commissioned from a carefully selected supplier, had invested in the appropriate presentation equipment and had appointed a newly joined secretary – a fairly junior staff member – to be responsible for its operation. The result was a number of highly successful, smooth-running presentations which owed their effectiveness not only to the quality of the programmes, but also to the enthusiasm and commitment of the equipment operator. The moral of the story is: people are often much more important than sets!

LIGHTING

If it's bad it can ruin the event; if it's good, no one notices it. Lighting is a facility that's easy to forget – '. . . so long as the audience can see what's happening the lighting's OK, isn't it?' – but it's one of the most powerful design tools an organiser can have. Even when the budget won't run to a decent set or when the venue is particularly dispiriting, a good lighting designer can often save the day, creating an environment that makes the place look good even though it isn't.

Designing and installing a large lighting rig is beyond the capabilities of most in-house organisers or producers – but they should all be aware of the very important part lighting plays in the design process.

Light is the medium used to paint an event. The skilled lighting specialist – who may not only work closely alongside the designer but may also be the same person – can use lights to create moods in just the same way a painter will use colour. One look at the size and complexity of a lighting rig for a large conference should be enough to tell you that this is a specialist area and one not to be dabbled in.

With smaller events, on the other hand, an in-house team might well tackle the job using the bare minimum of equipment aided by a liberal dose of common sense. Where is most light needed? Who or what is the focal point of the event? Is ambient light necessary to enable delegates or students to take notes? Asking these and other questions, plus a little trial and error, should enable you and your team to devise a lighting design which doesn't draw attention to itself and which allows everyone to get on with the job in hand – in other words, a design that works.

What can it do?

Illuminating an area with light of varying strengths and qualities can change its character; what was dark and gloomy can become light and joyous; what was bare and uninteresting can become rich and mysterious. Lighting also plays a vital role in providing participants in the event with an environment in which it's easy to work – it helps if they can see to read their scripts, for example! How the lighting plot is devised to provide these features depends upon the size and nature of the event – and what lighting is already available.

Venue lighting

The lighting available in hotels is generally unsuitable for larger events, although organisers of seminars and small group meetings may find it possible to use the existing lighting.

It's quite often important to discover whether it's possible to black-out the area. Slides or overhead projector transparencies are best viewed in semi, if not complete, darkness so it's necessary to find out how to achieve that state – by drawing curtains or screens across windows, for example.

If the event needs lighting equipment which has to be brought in and installed, make sure the building is structurally able to accept it. Lighting a large event often involves installing a lighting grid – a heavy frame upon which the lights are mounted – and this frame may be suspended from the ceiling or walls of the venue. Bringing together the designer and lighting designer (who may well be one and the same) with the venue manager at an early stage in the planning process should help to avoid problems here. With larger lighting rigs it will also be necessary to establish whether the venue's electrical supply is capable of providing the power needed. An otherwise very successful event at a large hotel I once attended was somewhat marred when the spectacular sound and light display which provided the grand finale blew several fuses and plunged the room – and indeed most of the hotel – into darkness. Once again, early discussions between lighting designers and venue management representatives can establish what is possible and what isn't.

Lighting large events

If your event is big enough to need a large lighting rig it will probably be taking place in a fairly large space, one of the bigger hotels perhaps, or a purpose-built conference centre. In either of these cases – almost certainly with most conference centres – facilities to handle large lighting rigs will be available or the rig itself will be in place, probably with many lights already attached – although lighting designers always seem to need a few more. The facilities and staff at most UK conference centres are accustomed to the demands made by huge events, so however vast or outlandish your lighting scheme it can probably be handled.

As soon as the venue location has been decided and the event is beginning to take shape, the organiser, the designer and the lighting designer should get together to plan lighting requirements. With a small event this might simply mean the organiser writes a note reminding himself that drapes will be needed to cover a window, or an adjustable desk lamp would help speakers see scripts more clearly, for example. With larger events many of the potential problems will be technically beyond the average organiser's competence but providing he or she communicates well with the lighting expert on the production team or with venue staff no difficulties should be experienced.

Lighting do's and don'ts

- Don't put too much strong lighting on to speakers; it can make them hot and uncomfortable as well as making it difficult for them to read a script or autocue.

- Do make sure the venue is suitable for your lighting plan. Some venues object to heavy lighting rigs being attached to walls or ceilings.

• If you're videotaping the event, do ensure there's sufficient lighting to enable the camera to capture a good quality image. Although modern video cameras have improved tremendously over the past few years, some still demand fairly high light levels to capture a decent image. This can result in a set that has to be flooded with light, effectively drowning out any subtlety of design you might wish to have featured. Only two solutions exist here; buy or borrow the best, most sensitive video camera you can; or arrange to shoot the event at a dress rehearsal so the audience doesn't have to suffer the lighting overload.

• Don't forget that darkness can be effective too. If the venue can be blacked out completely it could provide a useful dramatic effect.

• Do remember a reading light for speakers. These are often built into lecterns, but it's a good idea to take a small, portable lamp to be on the safe side.

• Don't let your staff or delegates touch professional lighting rigs or equipment. The consequences could be expensive, dangerous or both.

• Do treat lighting as an integral part of conference or event design, rather than an 'add-on' technique. By itself, lighting can create an environment and could help save on set construction costs; so talk to the lighting specialist and designer together, if they aren't one and the same person.

DESIGN – IN-HOUSE OR BUY IN?

It's very unlikely that you employ anyone in your company with the necessary skills to design all the elements of a large conference. You may have people with special DTP expertise, however, and providing the conference design theme is followed it should be possible to produce good print material and show substantial cost savings. In general though, it's best to acknowledge the vital importance of design to the success of your event; to recognise that you will usually be unable to find the necessary design skills within your company; and to buy in the best you can afford. The expense will be worth it.

7 TECHNICAL FACILITIES

● Definitions   ● Prompting devices   ● Information
support   ● Slides and transparencies   ● What is AV?
● Overhead projector (OHP)   ● Video   ● Theatrical
effects   ● Sound   ● The use of technical
equipment

Perhaps the most effective conference of all would be the one in which the top person – the managing director, chief executive, chairperson or whoever – walks into a pool of light on a bare stage then, without notes, teleprompt, or technical support of any kind, delivers a thirty-minute speech which instructs, informs and delights a packed house with its profundity, its sparkle and its wit.

Some leading businesspeople can do this, of course, and so can many professional actors, which is why many of them earn a good living on the conference circuit, adding not only a great deal of entertainment value to corporate events but also the vital human touch.

But the ability to deliver this kind of 'performance' isn't one that all businesspeople have or, indeed, need to have. Pinning responsibility for the success of an event so firmly to one person isn't such a good idea in any case, and the load is usually shared by developing a structure that relies on other features to inform, motivate and entertain audiences – features often provided by technical facilities.

DEFINITIONS

In the conference and event context, technical facilities can be defined as any equipment which aids the delivery and understanding of a message. From the audience's point of view – the only point of view that matters – the nature and function of the equipment isn't important, although its effect is. The maximum effect can best be achieved by the seamless integration of technical facilities into the event – they should never appear to be 'stuck on' just to impress – and it therefore follows that spending a great deal of money on elaborate and expensive equipment to dazzle your audience may not achieve any useful long-term goals. It's relatively easy to stun an audience with a display of technical brilliance, but it's another thing to ensure that audience remembers a message. Any technical facility used for an event should aid the process of communication, not become an end in itself; the medium is *not* the message here!

Whether you're planning a seminar for a small group or a product launch for an audience of hundreds you'll almost certainly be using technical facilities of one sort or another. In this chapter we'll look at some of the facilities commonly used and briefly describe what they do, how they work and how best to use them.

PROMPTING DEVICES

A speaker with head permanently bowed down to a fistful of notes while addressing an audience is not likely (a) to be heard nor (b) warmly received. 'If he can't remember it, how does he expect us to?' is a frequent cry which, although unfair to someone who isn't a professional speaker, is at least understandable when that speaker is usually asking his audience if they'll be good enough to remember his message.

There's nothing quite so impressive as delivering a statement or a message looking straight into the eyes of an audience, apparently speaking from memory, perhaps even from the heart, and that's what a prompting device allows a speaker to do. Originally developed for television – hence the name teleprompt

– these devices work by reflecting lines of type from a hidden TV screen on to a sheet of glass mounted at an angle in front of the speaker. In television the glass is mounted close to the camera lens which is focused on the speaker so it doesn't 'see' the words; similarly, in the conference version the angled glass is too small and too far from the audience for it to notice the lines of type the speaker can see quite plainly.

The advantages of the teleprompt are self-evident. You can hold your head up and thus be heard more clearly; you can look the audience straight in the eye so giving a stronger impression of sincerity; and because you no longer have to remember words, you can concentrate on your delivery, emphasising all the right words and phrases to make your speech even more effective.

There are few disadvantages. Occasionally a speaker will find it difficult to read from a teleprompt screen – although an adjustment to the room or set lighting usually cures the problem – and some speakers feel a prompting system ties them to a set speech, leaving little room for ad libbing. In practice, the experienced teleprompt operators who come with the hired equipment and who prepare the script for the system can make changes right up to the minute a speech begins – once, in my experience, changes were made to the end of a speech as the speaker was on his feet and half-way through its delivery.

The teleprompt system's great benefit is that it can give a speaker confidence. If the script is reasonably well written, if it says what you want it to say and you are happy saying it that way, and if it's been rehearsed a few times, you should feel secure enough to depart from the words appearing in front of you and ad lib a little. The teleprompt operators are accustomed to this so they'll simply pause the script until the speaker decides to return to the scripted speech.

A number of companies offer teleprompt systems for use in the conference field – a list of some of them appears at the end of this book in the Technical Facilities section. All these companies offer similar systems, perhaps the only difference between them being the varying levels of efficiency and cheerfulness of the operators.

Speakers new to the teleprompt system usually become accustomed to it very rapidly – and wonder how they ever managed without it. Most of the teleprompt systems companies will give advice on training speakers to use the system and, although it can't make a poor speaker into a scintillating performer, it can give even the most nervous and inexperienced a sense of security and confidence. If there are many speakers in an event, or if it's vital for a key speaker to make the best possible impression, consider using a teleprompt system; it can make all the difference.

INFORMATION SUPPORT

Sometimes even the best script or the most efficient prompting system can't help a speaker find the right words. When there's a question to answer – from a shareholder at an AGM for example – a speaker needs to have information instantly available if a quick and knowledgeable reply is to be made. The problem here is that information usually comes in printed form and so much printed paper would be needed to cover every eventuality it would be impossible to access any of it quickly.

One answer to this problem was pioneered at the London AGM of a large UK company. The chairman and his fellow directors sat behind the usual AGM desk, into the top of which had been built a number of VDUs. These were linked to a video disk unit backstage loaded with a specially prepared disk containing literally thousands of facts and figures on the company, and its performance. Many of these were in graphic form, often taken from company publications and designed to be easy to understand at a quick glance.

The video disk – like the CD used in music systems – offers fast random access times so any part of the information stored on the disk can be reached and displayed within seconds. All that had to be done was to index the disk information with codes given to key words or phrases. When a shareholder mentioned one of the key phrases – 'overseas performance' for example – the code was keyed into the video disk player's computer – and within two or three seconds the visual information appeared on the VDUs in front of the platform speakers.

Expensive certainly, for the production of a master video disk is a complex specialist process. But the speed with which the chairman and his colleagues responded to questions, and the ease with which they quoted facts and figures, was most impressive – and as most of the graphic material used already existed as artwork for other company publications, and the disk itself went on to be used in company information points and at exhibitions, the great image boost this system gave the company in fact cost it very little.

SLIDES AND TRANSPARENCIES

We'll call 35mm transparencies 'slides', because that's what they're usually called and 35mm is the size almost invariably used; the large sheets of acetate used to project information in the form of graphs or text on to a screen from an overhead projector (OHP) we'll call 'transparencies'.

For many years the 35mm slide was the mainstay of the conference world. Using the ubiquitous Kodak 'Carousel' slide projector, first singly or in pairs, later in computer-controlled massed banks of up to 100, slides were not only capable of making complex subjects and processes comprehensible – they could also provide truly spectacular visual displays.

WHAT IS AV?

The practice of using slide projectors linked to sound systems first became known as slide/tape naturally enough; later it took on the rather misleading name audio-visual or AV – misleading because AV is a generic term for a range of media including film and video, rather than the sole province of slide/tape enthusiasts. Whatever it's called, the secret of AV's success was and is simple; a subject appears to 'move' if two or more projectors successively throw slightly different images of it on to the same screen area. Graphs can be made to 'grow', charts can develop on screen, complex processes can be demonstrated in simplified action while the sound tape accompanying the visuals not only provides a voice, music and effects track, but also, on early equipment, a separate track carrying pulses to activate the slide changes.

AV first came into its own with twin projector units, often available in 'portable' form – although 'transportable' would have been a better term, considering the size and weight of the boxes. These twin projector set-ups could produce three visual effects.

1. A cut, in which one picture was rapidly replaced by another. This abrupt transition might indicate a change of pace or subject and could allow for some fast-moving sequences. On early equipment it was only possible to change pictures every two or three seconds, however, so 'fast-moving' is a relative term.

2. A dissolve, produced by gradually fading down one image on screen while gradually fading up another. It was possible to select the dissolve speed – from a brisk three seconds to a leisurely nine seconds – and given good photographic images, ideally shot with a pin register camera to ensure images matched precisely, the dissolve could produce magical effects. A scene might be transformed from day to night, 'before' and 'after' graphically demonstrated, or titles super-imposed over a scene – and all this accompanied with appropriate music, sound effects and commentary. It was 'the movies' but without a movie budget!

3. Then there was the coyly named 'twinkle' effect. While one image remained stationary on screen, the other projector was switched rapidly on and off, superimposing its image on to the picture displayed on screen. At its simplest, this effect could, for example, produce arrows 'pointing' to critical parts of a diagram or a machine – or it might be used less seriously to 'jazz up' a visual display.

Those were the only three effects available to AV practitioners in the early two-projector days and I have detailed them here simply because they were in essence the basis of all the AV developments that followed.

115

AV development

The one major advantage AV has over all other visual media is the superb, unmatchable quality of a good 35mm transparency projected through professional equipment on to a large screen; there is, at the time of writing, still nothing to touch it. The one major disadvantage of AV in its early days was that however marvellous these images were, they didn't move, or at least, they didn't move fast enough.

Then came the computer, and with it ways of controlling not just one or two projectors but as many as were considered necessary or desirable. Although slide projectors were still speed restricted – the mechanical business of slide changing still takes around a second – linking a large number of them together made it possible to change screen images very quickly indeed. This led to the interesting theory that twenty-five or more projectors all trained on the same screen area should be capable of changing the screen image twenty-five times in a second – thus producing movies! It's a theory some AV producers seem to have been intent on proving over the past few years, to the detriment of the medium I believe. To be sure, it's possible to 'animate' AV to achieve movie speeds quite effectively, but it's a facility that should be used sparingly if at all; the complexity of the process, the equipment required and the time taken to achieve the result turns AV into an expensive medium when one of its charms has always been its economy; and, what's more important, the superb quality of AV's screen images – the medium's greatest advantage – goes largely to waste.

AV today

AV offers today's conference organisers two major abilities; it can enable them to present or explain difficult or complex subjects with clarity; and it can provide a visually exciting backdrop to an event. For example, a seminar organiser might find a twin projector AV presentation useful to define the ground rules for a subject before embarking on a discussion; while the organiser of a product launch or an AGM could use AV not only to inform but also to impress an audience, one part of the event using the medium's graphic ability to promote understanding, the other its powerful facility to impress with spectacular displays of colour, light and sound.

Until AV began to aspire to the condition of the movies it was an economic medium – indeed, it still is for organisers aware of its true qualities. A good script – one that isn't too wordy, allowing the pictures to do most of the work – excellent photography by a specialist in the medium, the intelligent use of sound and the services of a producer who knows how to construct a sequence in sound and vision are the major ingredients in an effective AV programme and although they aren't – or shouldn't be – cheap, they do give very good value for money. The combination of very high quality images, perhaps transformed photographically on a rostrum camera before being expertly edited together, a superb soundtrack – imaginatively created by sound engineers, almost invariably in the highest quality stereo – and a persuasive and well-thought out script is one that can solve a great many conference communication problems. The fact that the medium can also be used to create a species of exciting wallpaper shouldn't blind anyone to its real value; AV can explain or clarify, impress or motivate, persuade or entertain just as effectively as almost any other communication medium, but far more economically.

AV has other benefits to offer. Common international technical standards mean that an AV programme made for the UK can also be shown anywhere in the world using the same equipment; updates are easy, providing the soundtrack doesn't date – you simply reshoot and replace slides; and because the pin register shooting technique allows movement to be simulated very economically, AV can also provide an effective substitute for more expensive video. A well-known London store has recently run a series of TV advertisements using this technique.

AV to video

AV can also travel well. Because the image quality is so good, AV works particularly well when the pictures are high, wide and handsome – which often means using a wide-screen format and many projectors. Because it would be expensive to duplicate this multi-projector and wide screen set up in another location, it's often possible to copy the AV to video, usually on the VHS format, allowing the programme to be seen on conventional closed-circuit TV equipment anywhere. AV purists usually bemoan the loss of picture quality resulting from the transfer, but the loss is usually only noticeable by those who've seen the original 'big screen' programme. Transferring to the small screen does cause a drop in quality, certainly, particularly if the original programme was made for an extra wide format, but the loss is usually well worth accepting when it allows the programme to be seen in other locations.

OVERHEAD PROJECTOR (OHP)

A device that simply transfers a typed or written image from an acetate sheet through a lens and magnifies it on to a screen, the OHP is a kind of modern blackboard, offering speakers the ability either to present ideas to an audience in pre-prepared OHP transparency form or to write them on to an acetate roll as the thoughts occur – or both methods together.

OHP transparencies are roughly A4 in size, which often leads to the temptation to simply type the information on to a sheet of A4, then photocopy it on to the acetate. All too often the result is an OHP that contains far too much information – a maximum of fifteen to twenty words is about right – and is virtually unreadable because the letters are too small. Lettered OHP transparencies are best made with a special thermal transfer machine, the originals being prepared using large characters from one of the dry transfer ranges or stencils.

OHP was once regarded as the poor relation of 35mm slides; although it offered speakers the ability to project written comments on to a screen instantly, the largely 'home-made' quality of the visuals commonly produced for OHP gave it a slightly amateurish air. The arrival of colour photocopiers and computers has changed that perception, however, and now very professional results can be achieved using computer-generated graphics printed either on to plain paper and subsequently photocopied in colour, or laser-printed directly on to the acetate.

VIDEO

If there ever was any difference between television and video it's disappeared almost completely now, certainly in the conference world. The miniaturisation of equipment has been responsible for the merging of the two disciplines, a merging which probably began when broadcast television companies started to use portable, lightweight video cameras and tape equipment to capture news stories. Today it's possible to go into a high street shop and buy incredibly sophisticated video equipment which, theoretically at least, brings the production of high quality video programmes within everyone's reach. Automatic exposure control, colour balancing, motorised zoom lenses – all these and many more features may make amateur camera operators or programme makers confident they can compete with the best – but, as ever, there's more to programme-making than simply having the right equipment. Whatever the medium, putting a good programme together is a complicated process, quite often involving a lot of hard work – something you won't discover reading advertisements for the latest home video equipment.

Video quality standards

Organisers considering the use of video should be aware that the audience will be more than usually critical if the quality they expect is not delivered; they will all be making comparisons with the material they see on their television screens every day. Creatively and technically, broadcast television standards in the UK are extremely high and the general public has come to expect the same standards whenever a video programme – or moving pictures of any kind – are seen. This same general public – who may be strongly represented in your audience – has very little idea of television and video production processes, however; 'Can't be all that difficult – looks easy enough on the telly, doesn't it?' seems to be the general view – borne out by a request I once had to give a quotation for videotaping an open air evening performance of *A Midsummer Night's Dream* for a client who plainly thought the venture was simplicity itself and thus bound to be extremely inexpensive. I had to point out to

119

him that if he wanted a good, watchable result at least three cameras would be necessary, that extra lighting would have to be used, and that a shooting script would need to be produced and some camera rehearsals undertaken. As I suspected, the estimated budget shocked the client – who left in a good, old-fashioned dudgeon remarking that he thought it only needed one camera stood at the back!

Advantages and disadvantages

Using prerecorded video sequences in the conference context can be a very economic way to add a lively sense of immediacy to an event. Leading company or industry figures who can't be present can put in an appearance on video; 'real-life' customers can comment on products or services – the well-known 'vox pop' technique; and those same products or services can be shown in action, in detail, over and over again or in slow motion, depending upon the needs of the producer and the audience. All these are big advantages for video, adding to that extra advantage of being an extremely familiar medium, one that most people readily accept.

The disadvantages? Video picture quality can't begin to match a projected 35mm slide – but neither can AV hope to capture live action so excitingly, so it's all square. But if really big images are needed video can have difficulty in reaching acceptable quality standards. The problem is that video images can't be projected in the same way as 35mm slides. The picture on a colour television screen comes from three colour 'guns' firing red, green and blue signals on to the face of the screen only a few inches away; to amplify and fire these signals on to a much larger screen which may be some distance away involves an inevitable quality loss however it's done.

There are three techniques commonly used to increase the size of video images.

● Self-contained video projection units house the videotape player, the projection unit and a large screen. These units may be positioned in the most effective location and are suitable for audiences of up to perhaps fifty people.

- Projection video units allow much larger images to be projected across greater distances. The projection unit is often bulky and requires some time to set up. A number of different systems are available; their effectiveness varies and all require expert technicians to operate them. Suitable for audiences of perhaps 100 upwards, these systems are often used for larger conferences and AGMs.

- The video wall is, strictly speaking, not comparable with the other two systems, because its aims are somewhat different. The video picture is divided by a grid, each part of the grid feeding a signal to a separate television screen. The result is a huge reproduction of the original picture on as many TV screens as the producer desires – or can afford. The effect is startling, an eye-catcher – which is why the technique is often used at exhibitions and similar events.

Video effects

As with AV, it's possible to manipulate video images so as to create visual effects. Where AV images are treated photographically, video is given the electronic treatment, the visuals being played through an effects desk which allows the original picture to be changed in literally hundreds of different ways.

For some years video facility companies throughout the land have competed furiously with one another to offer clients the latest and best video post-production facilities – including the latest, most versatile editing and effects equipment.

As a result of all this competition, clients now have an almost unlimited choice of ways to transform original video images – if they can afford it and if they can control the process.

Sophisticated effects equipment is expensive, clients must have the latest, the most sophisticated – *ergo*, clients must have the most expensive. It's a ridiculous equation, but that's how it often seems to work! In fairness, the quality of visual effects available is superb and a very great deal of creativity can be found inside the facility houses specialising in this work – but the fact remains, it's expensive.

Whether you want or need to use many video effects depends

upon the event you're organising and the expectations of your audience. Once again, these expectations will have been honed by television viewing, where TV commercials provide an excellent visual anthology of the latest fashions in effects. Audiences today are by and large visually very sophisticated – they may not know how a visual effect is done or what it's called, but they'll almost certainly recognise it as establishing some sort of credential for the ad or programme in which it appears. Like costume jewellery, if an effect is well chosen it'll make anyone look good; if it isn't, then even the most attractive programme is in danger of looking dowdy and just a trifle cheap.

Video terminology

The language used in post-production facilities may come as a surprise to many event organisers with little experience of the medium. It's not that it's excessively blue or profane – it's just that it might seem incomprehensible. A world in which flips, rolls, wipes and mosaics are commonplace can be unnerving, but it's a problem that must be faced if you're to get the best from the time you'll spend inside the edit suite. Once, when moving pictures meant film, it was possible to enter an edit suite confidently, knowing only the words cut, mix and fade. Then video arrived and with it the first video editors – who were almost always engineers too. As they invented strange new things for their machines to do they gave them strange new names; the snag was that they tended to keep these names to themselves and no one ever thought of publishing a list for the benefit of clients. Today that list would cover many pages – and there would almost certainly be a great deal of disagreement between the post-production houses on the precise meaning of some of the terms. The moral here is either to be absolutely certain you know what you want before you enter the edit suite; or to have absolute trust that your editor will do the very best he can with the material you give him. The production of a storyboard would be an ideal way to achieve the first option; as for the second, only your intuition can guide you – although in my experience editors are only too keen to deliver the best work they can; it's what makes clients come back for more, after all.

Live video

You might want to shoot a videotape record of your event; or you may decide to use video cameras to inject 'live' inserts into the programme. Either way, don't forget that even though modern video cameras are incredibly sensitive and will do a good job in fairly low light levels, the best-quality results will only be achieved if the lighting is good – which may mean running a video test in the location itself and installing supplementary lighting if it's needed. When shooting for the record, particularly if the event is a large one, bear in mind the *Midsummer Night's Dream* tale mentioned earlier; more than one camera will be needed, almost certainly extra lights – and rehearsals are advisable.

In-house help

Modern video equipment is, as they say, user friendly. Anyone can pick up a camera, point it in the right direction and get a viewable picture. If the budget is tight the temptation can be strong to give some of the technical work – camera operation for example – to in-house people. Succumb to it to a certain extent – getting staff involved in the nuts and bolts of a production is a great way to build a production team – but do spend sufficient time and effort rehearsing the team to make sure everyone knows what he or she is doing and why. Saving money shouldn't mean cutting corners.

As far as video post-production work is concerned, your company is unlikely to possess the equipment necessary for this work or to have staff with the skills required to carry it out. The organiser, the producer or the director – whatever you call him, the person responsible for the quality and content of the event – will therefore need to select a post-production facility and enter into a close working relationship with it. A list of post-production facility companies is found on pages 207–8 and 216–18.

THEATRICAL EFFECTS

It was once rumoured that the members of an aggressively *avant garde* pop group who consistently failed to make money from their loud and spectacularly awful music were doing very nicely thank you by hiring out their laser equipment to conference producers. At one time no self-respecting product could be launched without several shafts of laser light scything the air as an accompaniment. Once described as '. . . basically, a very expensive blue light', lasers are irrelevant, pointless, a waste of money – and totally essential for certain grandiose events where going over the top is not only expected but positively welcomed. Now somewhat out of fashion, it's still best to check your budget before ringing the laser people. (Some possibilities are given on pages 209–10.)

Given the right venue, adequate facilities and an event that calls for some degree of theatricality, almost every stage device is available. Atmospheric clouds of dry ice may be generated, gauze drapes and artfully positioned lighting can create effective illusions, lifts and revolves may be used where present or installed specially for the occasion – and never forget the amazing power of sound.

Sound

In an industry that professes some skill in the audio-visual media, it's always surprising to find how often the audio bit is forgotten. While it may be true that audiences remember 70 per cent of what they see but only 30 per cent of what they hear, the power of music, of words and of sound effects is surely undeniable and, combined with the right visual images, unbeatable.

There is so much to choosing and using music and voices that it would almost certainly fill a separate book. Chapters might include advice to writers on the importance of writing for a known voice; on the use of silence as a powerful audio stimulus; on the acoustic difference between an empty space and a space full of people; and on sound effects as a kind of music.

It might also examine some technical aspects of sound. For example, although the stereo effect is well known, the unnerving sensation produced by a pair of out-of-phase loudspeakers is less familiar and well worth exploring. To try it, simply reverse the speaker leads on one loudspeaker and play a disc or tape that has a very well-defined 'central' sound image.

Our imaginary book would also describe the general awfulness of the public systems found in most venues and advise organisers always to arrange for their own to be installed; and it might also tell of a moment in a most prestigious conference when a minister of the Crown got to his feet to begin a speech using a radio microphone. Instead of his smooth and sonorous tones, however, the audience suddenly heard a few hoarse obscenities from a London minicab driver whose radio frequency had clashed with the minister's.

The importance of good quality sound can't be stressed enough; music that's too loud and speakers who can't be heard rank together as major irritants and every effort should be made to avoid them. Once again, you'll be unlikely to find a skilled sound technician for your in-house production team, but there may be someone with a particular interest in music or sound reproduction who could be given responsibility for liaising with the sound studio you select. A list of such studios and information on agencies dealing with voice-over artistes is on pages 204–5.

THE USE OF TECHNICAL EQUIPMENT

This chapter has attempted to cover some of the major types of technical equipment found in the conference world. It isn't possible to go into detail on all the equipment available because (a) there's so much of it, and (b) it's developing and changing all the time. There are some general points that can be made about the use of technical equipment though, points that are likely to be applicable whether you're producing a big budget product launch or a small-scale conference or seminar.

● *Book equipment in good time*
Popular equipment can be in short supply during the conference season, so order as early as you can. If you're using in-house equipment make sure it's available when you want it.

● *Hire equipment only from reputable suppliers*
As the day of the event approaches and you find yourself without a key piece of equipment, the temptation to hire it from a somewhat shady operator who's the only source available can

become irresistible. Resist it. Better still, avoid getting into this position by reading the above.

• Check the equipment well before the event

Even though you've hired your equipment from the most reliable company in town, check it – and keep checking it, right up to the moment you use it. A colleague was recently visited in his office by a salesman who skilfully persuaded him to watch a demonstration of the latest, greatest piece of computer software. 'He made it sound so attractive I would have bought it,' said my friend, 'But he had some problem with his machine – the mouse wouldn't work – so I rather lost interest.'

• Insist on adequate technical rehearsals

Speakers may wish to use every available moment of rehearsal time, but point out that their efforts will be worthless if the equipment is unreliable or breaks down.

• Choose technical operators with care

Ideally, use trained operators. If you're using in-house staff, devote some time to training them yourself or ask your equipment supplier to do this.

• Have a Plan B

Work on the assumption that *something* will go wrong and prepare for the most likely disasters. Have spare bulbs for the projectors, spare fuses for electrical equipment, a plentiful supply of gaffer tape (strong, black, highly sticky tape that's good for everything from attaching microphones to stands to fixing bits of scenery together) – and don't forget a torch!

Organising and producing a conference is an activity that's becoming increasingly complex and technically oriented. It's worth remembering, though, that however ingenious the equipment, however brilliantly it performs its role, the objective of the event is to communicate a message to the audience. If this objective isn't achieved then the event – and the equipment – will have failed.

Some events may not need a great deal of technical support. If you're lucky enough to be organising a conference for the person mentioned at the beginning of this chapter, someone who can hold an audience with his or her authority and charm, then the only technical concerns you should have are to make sure the sound system is working and to put your star speaker in a suitable pool of light. Other events, not blessed with such talent, will need more technical help to keep the audience involved and interested. As organiser, a part of your job is to decide just how much of that technical help is necessary – always remembering that the equipment and techniques you do use must be dedicated to one single aim: delivering the message effectively.

8 Producing
A CONFERENCE

● Sole control ● The checklist ● Rehearsal
● Speaking in public ● Full rehearsal ● Directing
personality speakers ● The event ● And afterwards ...

Organising an event such as a conference or a seminar really divides itself into two parts. There are the technical aspects to consider – what equipment you need, where it's to come from and who's to operate it; and then there's the human element – will the speakers be able to convey their messages effectively and is the audience in a suitable environment to receive those messages?

As the day of the event comes closer, these factors loom large. No longer are you dealing with words and designs on paper; now you've seen the venue, the script is taking shape and you realise there's a real space to fill, an environment to create and people to encourage, inspire or motivate if the event is to be successful.

If you're using a specialist conference production facility much of this work will be done for you – although as someone who is probably in frequent contact with event speakers you can play a vital role in encouraging them and liaising with the production facility if there are queries or problems. If you're 'going it alone', however, it's at this stage you really begin to feel the pressure build up.

SOLE CONTROL

Throughout this book I have mentioned how necessary it is for one person to assume full responsibility for an event if it is to have a coherent shape and style. I hold to that view even though at this point in the production process it can seem as if there are simply too many elements for one person to juggle successfully. But it can be done. The 'Things To Do' list is a great help if it's planned as an integral part of the production process right from the start; and intelligent delegation of some of the work can take a great amount of the load from a harassed in-house producer's shoulders, particularly if he also has his normal company work to do.

An obsession with 'lists' might seem to be an occupational hazard of conference production, but when you're in sole control, lists, checklists, schedules, call them what you will, help you stay on top of the job, aware not only of what should be done, but who should be doing it and when.

THE CHECKLIST

The larger and more complex the event the more lists you'll need if you want to keep everything under control, but this doesn't mean you have to submerge yourself in paper. If you're delegating some of the work you won't need a great deal of detail on your list, simply a note of what needs to be done, the date the work must be completed and the name of the person responsible for it. Make it quite clear to everyone involved that they must tell you when they've completed a job on the list; if it isn't reported you can waste a great deal of time finding the person responsible and checking with them.

Some organisers use the checklist as a way of pulling a production team together, as a device which helps everyone see the job as a whole and realise the importance of their particular part in it. One way of doing this – if you have the space and the facilities – is to mount a large, white 'write-on' panel on a wall and divide it into a number of sections relating to the activities which need to be tracked. Asking the people responsible for various parts of the project to keep their own sections up to date not only provides a very effective method of progressing the work, but also keeps the whole production team in the picture and encourages them all to perform well.

The amount of detail you include in your checklist is up to you, but it's best to keep it simple; as mentioned above, What? When? and Who? are the only three questions the checklist has to answer. To make the whole process clearer, it's sometimes best to divide the project into sections – the venue technical equipment, speaker support material and so on – and make different people responsible for each of them. The organiser's own checklist, however, will contain everything and be strictly chronological – and as the day of the event approaches part of it may look something like the page opposite.

REHEARSAL

It's usually admitted that rehearsals are important. I'd go further and say they're probably more important than the event itself! You may have an exciting message to put across, a great script, a magnificent venue and all the technical backup you need, but until you try everything out with the people who'll be taking part in the event you won't know if its going to work the way you've planned.

Don't let anyone dodge a rehearsal – certainly not the final full rehearsal, although extenuating circumstances might just excuse absence from earlier run-throughs. Quite possibly the Chief Executive – or his PA – won't consider his presence necessary if he's seen and OK'd the script. After all, he's very busy. If anyone tries to escape rehearsal that way, you might gently point out that the event is important, that all the participants are devoting a considerable amount of time and effort to it, and that, at the very least, it would be polite to turn up for rehearsal like everyone else. If that doesn't work then perhaps you might spread the (true) story of a top company executive whose high-flying career was abruptly grounded after a disastrous showing at a company conference. While his colleagues stood confidently before their teleprompts, calmly detailing their future plans in perfect synchronisation with a series of crisp, clear slides, our man, unrehearsed, was clearly ill at ease with the teleprompt, made a nervous grab for the desk microphone into which he bawled extremely loudly and, to clinch matters, decided to

MARKETING DIVISION
Strategy Conference
Royal Hotel Banqueting Suite – 4 September 9.30 a.m.

By date:	Activity	Action
23/8	Finalise JB's script. He to sign final draft.	DR
24/8	Brief artist JB's support slides. (Delivery 30/8)	DR
24/8	Preview opening/closing AV modules.	AF
25/8	OK revise of Strategy Document. Pass to Production Dept for layout, coding and print.(Delivery 30/8)	CO
26/8	Check guest list responses (Hull/ Newcastle/Bristol/Edinburgh offices). Follow up on phone if necessary.	JF
27/8	Confirm car booking railway station – Royal Hotel for VIPs 18.15 3/9.	GM
27/8	Confirm accommodation booked at Royal – 2 doubles, 1 single. 3 – 5/9 inc.	GM
27/8	Confirm with Royal evening booking of Banqueting Suite 2/9 for rehearsal.	GM
30/8	Confirm AV equipment hire 2/9-5/9. Check delivery time 2/9!	AF
30/8	All scripts to Autoprompt. Confirm arrival and check autoprompt + operator available 2/9 and 5/9.	DR
30/8	Reminder memos + phone calls to all participants: full rehearsal 17:00 2/9.	AF
30/8	Contact Conference Manager at Royal - organise refreshments for 20, evening of 2/9. (NB: 3 vegetarians)	AF

depart from his script to deliver several off-key jokes, all of which went down like the proverbial lead balloon. If only he'd come to rehearsal!

Rehearsal timing and frequency

Time the holding of rehearsals so you get the maximum benefit from them. Hold them too early and by the time the event itself arrives everyone has forgotten the lessons learned; hold them too close to the event and a sense of panic can set in, along with a feeling that it's too late to make changes. With large events the early rehearsals and run-throughs can start up to a month or more before the event; depending on the proficiency of the speakers, rehearsing once or twice a week should be sufficient up to perhaps a week before the event. After that, once a day will keep everyone on their toes until the full dress rehearsal, perhaps the day before the event. Ideally, make it a morning rehearsal giving everyone the chance of a 'day off' – and the organiser an opportunity to make last-minute adjustments to equipment or material.

Changes

If rehearsals are going well, with speakers and technicians clearly relaxed and confident, now is the time to consider incorporating those tricky bits you might have dreamt up in the early planning stages, but dismissed as being 'too complicated'. Generally, uncomplicated, straightforward events have a far greater chance of success, so it's better to plan a structure that concentrates on delivering the message effectively rather than devising an overambitious plan that might work stupendously well – but could go disastrously wrong. 'Play safe' may seem a remarkably unadventurous motto, but bearing in mind the costs involved and the effort that goes into most events, it's one that's well worth adopting if you want to achieve some degree of success for your event, not only for yourself but for all the people who've devoted their time and effort to it.

The very first conference I directed taught me it was best to start simply. I had originally written the conference for someone else to direct and, knowing the strong capabilities of the director concerned, I hadn't spared the complications – it was quite a 'tricksy' event, but one I was sure he would pull off magnificently. A month before the event he rang me with the news that he'd had to withdraw and had nominated me to replace him. So off I went to the first rehearsal, opened the script – *my* script – and promptly realised with horror that it was far too complicated for me to handle. Remembering that awful feeling, ever since I've tried to write simple scripts that work as they are, but allow room for expansion or elaboration – if there's time and if the participants feel happy about it.

Technical rehearsal

If there's an appreciable amount of technical equipment involved in your event, you need a technical rehearsal before you ask your speakers to rehearse their lines and movements at the location.

A technical rehearsal checks three things:

- Is the director able to communicate his wishes clearly and effectively to the operators?

- Can the operators carry out these commands?

- Does the equipment work properly?

Most good technical direction is done on paper. If the script or the notes on the event are detailed enough and if the technicians or operators concerned have been involved from an early stage, by the time the technical rehearsal is called at the venue everyone should know precisely what is expected of them. The technical rehearsal then becomes a simple equipment test, plus a check that lines of communication are clear.

Lines of communication

A good channel of communication between the organiser/director and the technical crew is essential, and if it does nothing else, the technical rehearsal should enable you to set one up or iron out any snags in an existing channel. If the event is particularly large the director may need to exercise control over a number of technical facilities and he is likely to do this from a central control position. In the majority of purpose-built conference centres this would be a fully-equipped glass-fronted control room with a view over the 'action area', but in most other venues a space would have to be set aside for a control position and links would need to be established between it and the technicians. Visual links might do if the room is small enough and the light good enough for you clearly to see all the technicians; but if the event requires a dark or semi-dark environment and if the technicians are placed at widely-spaced intervals around it, you'll need to use some form of audio link. It's my experience that when audio links develop faults – as they occasionally do – they unerringly occur during the event itself and just when the link is most needed. So even though your audio links work well at rehearsal, it's advisable to have Plan B ready, just in case – the Plan B usually involving some form of visual signal that can be used to cue a technician if the audio link fails.

Don't rush the technical rehearsal. If there's time, try to run the whole event completely through so that everyone can become accustomed to the words being spoken and the verbal cues being given. Don't use the actual speakers for this however; they may become nervous if mis-cues or mistakes are made during the technical rehearsal. The director and/or members of the production team should, if possible, talk and walk the whole event through at least once for the benefit of the technical crew. And, once the technical rehearsal is over, let the technical crew take a break while the speakers are rehearsed – in fact, insist upon it. The speakers want privacy for their first run-through in the venue as much as the technicians do.

Speaker rehearsal

Before any speaker begins rehearsing a speech ask if he or she is happy with their script. If the speaker isn't it's pointless to continue and you'll have to break and sort out the problem or rehearse another speaker while someone else sorts it out. However, by the time you reach the final rehearsal stage –

usually the day before the event – all script problems should have been solved; indeed, if you're using some form of teleprompt they'll *have* to be solved, because the operators need to type the script into whichever system is being used and they usually do this a few days before the event.

Again, if there's time, try to rehearse each speaker at least once without any technical support – apart from the teleprompt system, if one's being used. The sincerity and force with which speakers deliver their words will do a great deal to ensure their message 'gets across', and by concentrating solely on voice delivery, tone and contrast the director can help speakers make the best possible contribution to the event.

SPEAKING IN PUBLIC

Some people are consumed with fear as they approach the job of addressing a group of fellow human beings. They worry that they're talking too loudly, not loudly enough, that people are looking at them or not paying enough attention, that their script makes them sound too stuffy or too childish or – the worst nightmare of all – that they'll suddenly lose their voice. The throat will dry up, the tongue become thick and unresponsive, and the speaker will simply stand there and croak unintelligibly. These fears can be overcome by encouraging the speaker to talk more slowly and – if using a microphone – more softly so as to gain confidence; and by changing the script to match the speaker's voice patterns so the words spoken are *the speaker's* words and thus more comfortable to say.

Incidentally, it's definitely not a good idea to try to do these things at the venue rehearsals. It's too late – you'll probably be rehearsing an event that will take place within one or two days at the most; and it's not kind to speakers who will have enough to do accustoming themselves to a much larger space, a different acoustic and, perhaps for the first time, all the paraphernalia associated with a conference or similar event.

What you should be doing at these venue rehearsals is to instil confidence into speakers. Just because they're in a different, larger space, there's no need for speakers to shout or make overexpansive gestures. If you're using microphones a good sound technician will increase the sound level for naturally quiet voices, and the way the event is lit will ensure that speakers can be clearly seen.

Speakers addressing a large audience without the benefit of amplification must of course be sure they can be heard distinctly by everyone present. The words must be delivered fairly slowly and deliberately, the speaker's head should be lifted so he is addressing the back rows of the auditorium and he should pitch the voice at a tone and level sufficient to carry to those back rows. To ask an untrained speaker to speak to a large audience without amplification is unwise to say the least. It's a job for a professional – an amateur will often simply shout, which is neither dignified nor effective. Most venues have some form of public address system installed, however, so the problem rarely arises; but if your large venue lacks such a system, either hire and install one of your own, or book your speakers into a voice training school.

Your speakers will almost certainly be using microphones, but you shouldn't have to ask them to learn correct microphone techniques – keep it simple and they'll keep relaxed. Make sure the microphone is easily adjustable so speakers can move it to let them speak comfortably without bending or stretching to reach it, then ask them to speak just a little louder than they would if they were speaking to one other person. Make sure they stand straight with the head raised, not buried in the script, and encourage them to relax and look around the auditorium from time to time, and not to keep the eyes fixed hypnotically on the same place.

Relaxing the speaker

Relaxing is one of the secrets of successful public speaking – in fact, it's probably *the* big secret. Here are just a few ways you might help your speakers achieve that cool, calm, relaxed appearance . . .

- Don't rehearse them right up to the last minute. Try to hold a final rehearsal several hours before the event, then leave them alone.

- If you can, make sure speakers get an early night. Some particularly nervous speakers stay up late, drink a little too much and perform badly the following day.

- Speakers should be dressed comfortably. No, not that shabby old cardigan, but a favourite suit or a comfortably worn-in pair of shoes can help a speaker feel at ease.

- Make sure all your speakers know how important it is to take their time in speaking. They don't have to slow to a crawl, but they do need to speak clearly and that's best done if they speak purposefully and deliberately.

- Make sure there's a glass of water on the speaker's rostrum. It's a very welcome sight for someone who's just about to 'dry-up' half-way through a speech.

- Have a supply of something a little stronger than water for the really desperate cases. Use with care, however!

- If there are speaker support slides, make sure your speakers have absolute faith in their correct and timely appearance. To achieve this, rehearse your technical crew until they squeak. Speakers must *not* be worried about technical matters.

- If necessary, organise some audience reaction at appropriate moments. To speakers, a silent audience is a hostile audience.

- And at all times the producer should exude complete and utter confidence. Not only the speakers but the whole production crew can benefit from this.

FULL REHEARSAL

Putting everything together at the final full rehearsal for an event is an exciting, if anxious, moment for everyone concerned, not least the organiser/director. It's essential to make this final rehearsal as realistic as possible. Put someone on the door leading into the room with strict instructions to admit no one. Recruit a small but vocal audience from the speakers' and technicians' friends and relatives, or from venue staff. And try not to break the tension by stopping simply to adjust a light or rerun a video clip or slide sequence; it's tension that drives an event along, lifting everyone into a state in which they often 'perform' far better than they – or anyone else – expected.

Time the event for future reference, make notes – a script layout that leaves a wide left-hand margin is helpful here – and if there are any last-minute adjustments or words of advice you want to give speakers, try to make your comments positive or, if that's not possible, be sure to make them in private. And at the end of the final rehearsal, even though you might have a sneaking feeling that there are a few things that could be greatly improved, you will, of course, exude confidence and calmness. Even after a successful rehearsal speakers and technicians can still be nervous and unsure, but if they see the person who's ultimately responsible for the event apparently unworried and cheerful it'll improve their confidence enormously.

DIRECTING PERSONALITY SPEAKERS

Your event may involve the appearance of a guest speaker, or it might have been structured around a personality. In either case if you're inexperienced in event direction you might spend a sleepless night or two wondering how you are going to tell this well-known industry figurehead or media star what to do. Don't worry; the people who offer themselves as guest speakers or compères in the conference and event market are almost in-variably completely professional people who know how to add value to any presentation. All you have to do is to discover what their strengths are – asking them is a pretty good way – then be flexible enough to accommodate those strengths within the event structure. Ideally, the scriptwriter will have met the per-sonality – or at least have a good knowledge of his or her strengths – and will have built these into the script, so much of the work will have been done for you. But the personality is usually as anxious as you are to make the event a success, so it's very rare to find serious conflict between personalities and event directors.

It is rare, but it's not totally unknown. What should you do if your guest star insists on ignoring your script and launches an attempt to restructure the event around his glittering personality? First, be ready with a pretty radical Plan B, one that allows you to mount the event without the personality. Next, try gentle persuasion, calling on the star to use every ounce of his professionalism to overcome the obvious limitations of the script, the venue and his fellow speakers. And if that doesn't work, get tough with the personality, insist he sticks to the script (which *was* sent to him weeks ago, wasn't it?) and threaten to dispense with his services if he won't or can't agree. One of my colleagues once reached the final stage of this risky process and reports a very bad-tempered climb-down by the personality – who then went on to deliver a magnificent performance of what was, in all honesty, a not particularly good script. 'You should have seen the icy smile he gave me afterwards,' said the colleague, 'As if to say "So there!"' But although it worked for him, it's definitely a path of last resort; appeals to the star's better nature and professionalism, although perhaps somewhat sneaky, are a less dangerous way of achieving the result you want.

THE EVENT

The audience is seated, the doors have been closed and the signal is given for the event to begin. Whether it's big or small, whether it starts with a straightforward speech by the Chief Executive or a spectacular video or audio-visual presentation, from this moment on you, as organiser and/or director, can only react to events, not shape them.

But there is a way you can exert some influence on the way the event is progressing; you can remain calm. Not only will the presence in their midst of someone so obviously relaxed encourage the other participants, if you can really keep thinking coolly and calmly you'll be much better prepared to meet an emergency should something go wrong.

But what can go wrong? Everything has been planned and revised, checked and double checked, run through time and again, there's just no way anything can divert the inexorable course of your majestic event – until a projector bulb blows, a backdrop falls down, or a tea lady enters a packed and expectant auditorium pushing a trolley with a squeaky wheel.

What corrective action you take to get the event back on

course depends not only on your cool reactions, but also very much on the nature of the calamity. The three real-life intrusions mentioned above were dealt with as follows. Blown projector lamps can happen at any time, technicians usually replace them in seconds – but the wise director checks that the technicians can do it in the dark, when the event's under way. These technicians could do it – and did.

The falling backdrop came as a nasty surprise to everyone. Held in position by heavy stage weights it was difficult to move – unless, like a speaker waiting to go on stage, you fell on to it. The speaker concerned had flown in from Europe that day and had no chance to rehearse – which is an excuse, not a reason, as one of my schoolmasters used to say. The director (me) could do nothing, but the day was saved by a quick-thinking technician who not only helped the speaker to his feet but lifted the backdrop into place single-handed – a feat for which he was awarded a round of applause from a generous audience. The moral: directors should appoint someone to shadow unrehearsed speakers if there's anything that can be tripped over, pulled down or ignited on set.

And the tea lady? It didn't happen to me – and I say that with some relief, because I don't know what I'd have done if it had – but apparently it came at an especially critical juncture when all eyes and ears were on a very senior person who had just begun to deliver a particularly serious speech. The tea lady's arrival not only ruined the mood, it brought the house down and although she was eventually persuaded to leave, by then the damage had been done. In retrospect it makes a good story – but it must be said that incidents like this shouldn't happen; a word to the caterers from the organiser of this event could have prevented it.

AND AFTERWARDS . . .

The event is over, the audience is preparing to leave and, if all has gone well, the organiser/director has received a vote of thanks. Before you head for the bar and a well-earned drink, however, there are a couple of things you still have to do.

First, try to assess the reactions of delegates or members of the audience. What did they like about the event, what did they dislike? Did the messages you were hoping to convey come across? And ask the participants if they have any comments to make on the way the event was handled. Were they rehearsed enough? Too much? Did they feel happy with the technical support they received? Note all these reactions carefully – write them down on the back of your script perhaps, or follow the example of one organiser I know who carries a small cassette recorder for the purpose – because these notes can be very useful when you're assessing the effectiveness of the event – and when you're planning the next one.

And, second, thank everyone – the speakers, the technical crew, the venue staff, the caterers – for the contribution they made to the event. Most conference events are 'one-off' affairs – unlike the theatre, your all-important first night is also your final performance – so the sense of anti-climax felt when the event is over can be quite severe. Thanking people for the efforts they've made over what was probably a fairly long period is not only a good thing to do, it should also help to lift everyone's spirits.

If the event has been marred by some ghastly error you'll no doubt wish to shout very loudly at the unhappy person who made the mistake. This is quite natural and I'd be the last to discourage you; it'll help relieve some pressure and it might even do the culprit some good if you can get him or her to understand where they went wrong. If you're faced with this sad necessity you will of course (a) make absolutely sure you're shouting at the right person and (b) shout in private, *not* in front of the assembled crew.

But let's hope there's no need for shouting and all your events end on a happy note, with everyone involved in the production gathering together – in the bar perhaps – where you can replay the highlights of your event as often as you like.

9 SPECIAL EVENTS

- Costs and objectives
- Technical equipment
- The road show
- PR coverage
- Venue choice
- Producing special events
- Incentive presentations
- Safety

Every event ought to be special, but the special events we're looking at here earn that title because they are unusual, either by virtue of the location in which they're held, or because they are unrepeatable, 'one-off' occasions which need a special combination of location, participants and ideas to make them successful.

COSTS AND OBJECTIVES

The 'specialness' of these events tends to make them expensive, which means they're generally more suitable for companies with fairly generous budgets. Unusual venues often cost more than the equivalent hotel space, transport costs can be high, and the presentation element itself will often require expensive technical facilities and expertise. But there are exceptions. By discovering a little-used venue or booking one out of season, or by creating the event around a simple but original idea, it's possible to minimise costs and for a special event to be staged for a fairly small audience at a reasonable price.

But why stage a special event in the first place? Probably for two reasons: because you want your audience to be impressed by your confidence and creativity; and because you need them to remember the event and connect it with a product or service you want them to buy. For example, if you're launching a new product and you need to gain the interest and goodwill of dealers or influential buyers you'd give them an exciting or unusual day to remember – hoping they'll remember your product as well. You would be unlikely to use that kind of special event to persuade your staff or workforce to remember new procedures or sales targets, however. The audience in this case should already have confidence in the company, and any extravagance in the choice of venue or style of presentation could be regarded with suspicion. Special events are, in general then, designed to impress and influence audiences from outside a company rather than internal groups.

Although it's by no means essential, staging an event in an unusual location is a popular way to give it a unique flavour. Special events are regularly held in historic buildings, a variety of striking or picturesque outdoor locations, not to mention specially-equipped conference carriages in trains, and boats ranging from river-bound motor launches to sea-going ships.

The organisers' choice of venue will usually be influenced by where they want to stage their event and how many people are expected to attend. If it's designed to attract many visitors from all over the UK then a fairly central location with good transport links – and plenty of car parking space – is indicated; on the other hand if the target audience is small, or if the size of the budget is not a major consideration, more out-of-the-way locations can be considered.

VENUE CHOICE

Everyone has his or her own way of starting the process of planning a special event – but many people begin by looking through a list of available venues to stimulate the imagination. You might have a good idea of the flavour the event should have, or perhaps you've already thought of a provisional title, in which case looking through a venue list is likely to crystallise your thoughts and enable you to start planning in earnest.

If you are using a specialist production facility to stage the event their staff with either be well aware of a number of suitable venues or will be in touch with organisations who provide venue information. You may decide to handle the venue choice yourself, in which case be prepared to spend some time visiting your short-listed venues to check that their sizes, facilities and attractions live up to their brochures. To be fair a brochure will rarely go out of its way to misrepresent a venue; it's simply that conference organisers are as much a prey to wishful thinking as anyone else and a venue's disadvantages may well fade mysteriously into the background if its positive features seem to fit the bill.

You may also have to consider hiring, converting or building a structure in which the event will be held. If you are simply hiring a tent or marquee there should be few problems – many reputable organisations will supply the structure, and will also advise on the installation of technical facilities in and around it. When it comes to converting an existing structure or building from scratch, however, unless you can call upon expert resources from within your organisation, don't try it. If you are contemplating the kind of event that requires a structure to be converted or built, it's likely to be a large-scale enterprise with a suitably large budget, so you shouldn't even be thinking of trying to save pennies by 'doing it yourself'. It's a highly specialised field and it's virtually certain you'll save money in the end by hiring experts to do this work for you.

A list of some production companies, venue finding organisations and facility companies who specialise in providing services for these events is found in the Directory of Suppliers starting on page 177.

SAFETY

Imagine. It's a warm, dry summer night and perhaps a hundred people inside a marquee are watching a spectacular product launch full of amazing technical effects. The marquee is packed not only with people, but also with a large amount of electrical equipment. There's an equipment malfunction – or someone drops a lighted cigarette – there's smoke and flame as fire breaks out – and suddenly there's panic, with a hundred people fighting to get out of the marquee and into the open air. What ten minutes ago was a successful event has turned into a potential disaster.

Over-dramatic? Perhaps. But when planning almost any kind of special event safety assumes great importance. Unlike a conventional event held inside a hotel or conference centre, a special event often breaks new ground, taking place at a location or in a structure which may conceal potential dangers. With the special event the organiser must take this into account by making every effort to ensure the safety of audience, speakers and technical staff. This may require a fairly rigorous system of audience control and the use of trained staff to supervise sectors of the audience in the event of an emergency; it may mean acquiring a familiarity with the laws concerning public safety; and, without being too alarmist about it, you must also take into consideration insuring against accidents causing personal harm or property damage. There are specialist insurance brokers who offer policies designed to cover the conference industry.

TECHNICAL EQUIPMENT

Special events generally demand the use of more equipment than conventional conferences. If the event takes place outdoors it's likely to be large and equipment needs – particularly lighting – are scaled up proportionately; and if the location has been chosen purely for its historical or theatrical qualities it may not have all the technical facilities needed so they'll have to be brought in. Ask yourself the following questions.

1. Does the venue have electricity – and, if so, does it have the capacity to handle all the equipment the event will need?

2. Will you need lighting? If so, how much?

3. What about sound?

4. Will you be able to show video or AV?

Electricity

With venues that can only provide conventional domestic electrics it may be safer to arrange a separate supply, either by running a line in from some nearby location or by installing portable generating equipment. Projectors, sound equipment and lighting can place a heavy load upon normal domestic electrical systems and the last thing you need is for all the fuses to blow just as the show reaches its climax. Venue owners don't appreciate this either. You should note, however, that big generators can be noisy, so if you intend using them make sure they can be situated out of earshot.

Lighting

Whether you need lighting or not will depend, of course, upon the nature of your event and its timing. The successful launch of a new car to a motor dealer audience on Plymouth Hoe took place at 11 o'clock one bright Wednesday morning, used a military band, a group of drum majorettes, a celebrity presenter, an aerobatic display by vintage aircraft – and no lights at all. In contrast, to promote a new product to the trade a multinational drug company staged an unforgettable evening of entertainment in the ruins of a West Country castle. *'Son et Lumière'* techniques were used but to promote a product rather than illuminate an historical event; a prerecorded voice-over linked the 'entertainment' sections; and marketing executives delivered product messages while projected images and lighting created powerful visual displays on the castle walls. No expensive bands, drum majorettes or vintage aircraft – just lights and sound, used creatively, holding an audience throughout a ninety minute presentation.

For an indoor special event you would check on lighting requirements in the same way as for a conventional event – but you'd remember that old walls, ceilings and electrical supplies might not be able to take the loads you may intend to impose upon them.

Sound

If your special event is taking place outdoors remember that (a) unamplified voices tend not to carry too well in the open air and (b) real life is noisy; in other words, the everyday sounds we filter out unconsciously – ambient noise like aircraft passing overhead, cars rushing past and so on – can assume horrifying proportions when we're consciously trying to listen to something important.

At most outdoor special events speakers' voices will almost invariably be amplified. To amplify a speaking voice so it may be heard clearly by dozens, perhaps hundreds or thousands of people is no simple matter however. Just making a voice louder won't do. What might be a comfortable sound level for listeners some distance from the loudspeakers could cause permanent injury to those a few feet away. This problem doesn't seem to concern fans at many pop concerts – although it should – but every person in your audience ought to be able to hear everything clearly, free of distortion, wherever he or she happens to be and without risk of injury – and this means using the best-quality professional sound equipment and professional sound engineers. Should you be in any doubt about this, ask yourself one question: 'If you had to choose between losing sound or vision during the event, which would it be?' However beautiful, witty or impressive your visuals, you can't beat talking to an audience, so it's imperative your sound system ensures they hear you 'loud and clear'.

Video and AV

If the event is being held outdoors and in daylight ambient light levels will make it difficult to show large screen images clearly, unless some form of canopy is built to shade the screen. When projecting slides some new screen materials now becoming available have surfaces which reflect light very efficiently so it's possible to achieve much better results than with conventional screens. Some modern video projectors can produce very good images too, and advances in electronic screens now make it possible to display huge video pictures – at a cost. And, in essence, cost is the answer to the question: whatever difficulties the venue presents, you'll almost certainly be able to show video or AV – if the budget will stand it.

One tip if you're mounting an outdoor event on a summer night and you're using slide projectors; beware the moths! Fluttering around in the projector lamp beams, they cast giant shadows on the screen which can, in extreme cases, spoil an otherwise perfect show. I would willingly pass on the solution to this problem – if I knew what it was!

PRODUCING SPECIAL EVENTS

It's unlikely the in-house organiser will have either the time or the ability to produce a special event all the way through from conception to performance; in any case, rather than becoming deeply embroiled in the details of this unfamiliar activity the in-house organiser will be much more valuable to the company doing what he or she was hired to do.

But the in-house organiser's decisions can exercise a good deal of control over some of the more important features of the event. Perhaps the most important decision is the choice of specialist production company or producer; the brief to them and their response to it should establish a firm partnership in which both partners are totally clear about their respective roles and are united in their desire to achieve the best possible result.

The exact balance of the organiser–producer relationship will depend upon many things – including the organiser's knowledge and ability in this field, and the tact and professionalism of the producer – but to strike the balance early on it helps if responsibilities are clearly defined.

For example, if there is to be a presenter, who chooses him or her? The specialist producer will no doubt have some ideas, almost certainly based on first-hand knowledge of the professional qualities of the people concerned. But the organiser knows his or her company and its character and is in the best position to choose who represents it.

Similarly, the choice of venue may be made by an organiser who is more concerned with corporate matters relating to the choice than to the technical or logistical problems it may present. The producer, on the other hand, may be familiar with another venue, know its qualities and be totally convinced it's the only possible choice.

In a good relationship both sides give a little and both sides win. If an organiser has the good sense to listen to the producer and to use his professionalism; and if a producer uses his ability to understand the client and his company and to put his needs first, both sides should profit from the relationship – and the event will be all the better for it. In other words, whatever problems may arise during the planning and production of a special event, if organiser and producer continue to talk to each other – better still, to communicate – all should be well.

THE ROAD SHOW

The road show may not really qualify as a special event, but anyone who has ever embarked upon a tour of the British Isles accompanying – not to mention occasionally mislaying – a truckload of display material and equipment will tell you it can certainly feel like it.

Whatever form a road show presentation takes, its planning and execution will inevitably involve many of the same operations as a special event. Venues will need to be researched, presenters hired, travel arrangements made, catering organised and so on – but there is a major difference; instead of just one event, several need to be organised. What is more, all of them are linked – if there's a hitch getting into or out of one venue, for example, the whole road show schedule could be affected, making it difficult to stage the later events on time.

Organising a road show can be a complex and time-consuming job, and with rare exceptions it's not one the in-house organiser can or should undertake. The road show is usually a touring version of an event originally staged close to the headquarters of a company, where the organiser can control the content and style. By the time the event goes 'on the road' it should have reached a high standard, there should be no need for full-time creative control to be exercised and the organiser can relinquish that part of the job. The other part – organising the venues, transport, crews and speakers – is best undertaken either by a freelance producer hired for the purpose or by contacting a production company with some experience in this field. Most of the larger production companies are regularly involved in road shows and are perfectly suited to this kind of work.

INCENTIVE PRESENTATIONS

These are often marketing events aimed at promoting goods or services rather than occasions for exchanging information, but the in-house organiser may be asked to make arrangements for them nevertheless.

If the incentive presentation is taking place as part of a larger event – a conference or exhibition perhaps – then it will be fairly easy to plan for its incorporation when the main event is being devised. If the incentive presentation is being staged alongside or close to the main event there's something to be said for giving it a slightly different character – using a design or colour scheme that's complementary, not identical, for example – rather than linking it in completely. Establishing the difference between the two events in this way can not only provide some entertaining contrasts, it can also give the audience a clear signal that both events have different aims, thus avoiding confusion.

'Self-standing' incentive presentations – those taking place under their own steam as it were, without the close proximity of another event – can make their own design rules, with the need to attract an audience being a major aim. If the presentation is to be made to members of the general public, promotional material will have to be prepared and this can echo the chosen design theme.

Choose the people who will staff your incentive presentation stand carefully. They not only have to 'sell' the products or services the stand is promoting, but also the company itself; their quality will be seen as indicative of your company's quality. And be prepared for a lively response to your event – be generous when estimating the number of brochures or free samples you'll need, for example. There's nothing more dispiriting than to have to turn potential customers away empty-handed.

PR COVERAGE

Whatever type of special event you're contemplating, its success will be measured not simply by the audience's reception of the event on the day itself. Special events aren't cheap and you are going to want every ounce of value from yours – which means preparing and executing a public relations programme.

Good PR coverage will generate interest in the event, your company and its products or services before, during and after the event itself. An in-house PR or publicity unit would almost certainly have the contacts and expertise necessary to carry out a thoroughly professional PR programme; though whether they always have the time or staff available is another matter.

Whether an in-house PR unit is used or an outside agency appointed, the organiser should take care to involve PR staff from the earliest stages of planning. While the organiser is concentrating on every single detail of the event, it's the job of the PR specialist to keep an eye on the wider world, to link your event with local or national happenings so that the target audience becomes aware of its existence as early as possible.

Once the PR machine is in motion it usually requires little input from the organiser, although any fuel he or she can provide is certain to be put to good use. I worked on one event where a middle-aged man who'd been seconded from his company job to drive the production unit's van, revealed he'd been a British boxing champion some years previously. The in-house organiser promptly telephoned the PR company handling the event – and the local paper ran a front-page story not only on the boxer, but also on the company in which he worked and the event they were about to hold.

The local press is just one of the avenues your PR team will explore. Contacts in the local radio station, regional TV and the trade press are all worth approaching; most of them are on the look-out for genuinely interesting items and if your event has something new to say to their audiences you stand a good chance of achieving coverage. With national press and TV you have to be very lucky indeed to get a mention – although inviting a Royal along to open the proceedings seems to be a guarantee of quite phenomenal press and TV coverage. If a Royal or a similar VIP accepts your invitation, be prepared for some hasty repositioning of company logos so they look well on TV! It's even worth talking to the camera operators to discover where they'll be shooting.

And, finally, don't forget that good PR begins at home.

Wherever you're staging the event, try to keep on good terms with local people or the staff of the venue you're using. It may not be easy – the strain of putting an ambitious special event together can be considerable – but if you can create a good impression with the locals you'll stand a good chance of doing the same with your target audience.

10 NEW TECHNOLOGIES

- Lasers • Slide projectors • Computers and CD-ROM
- The videophone • Teleconferencing • Interactive
video • Holography • Computer-generated graphics
- Video graphics • Summary

'It used to be so easy,' a colleague said to me recently, reminiscing on past conference exploits. 'You lit 'em nicely, made sure the speakers could see their words and then sent 'em all home happy with a rousing six-projector AV.' Although this was undoubtedly an oversimplified view of the conference process, I knew what he meant. Today, the business of communicating through the conference medium has become increasingly complex and refined, and although communication must remain the primary aim of all conferences, the techniques and tools used to achieve that aim are becoming more and more specialised.

Communications technology goes back a long way. If you drew a graph showing how improved communications have changed the world over the past few hundred years, the line would probably begin to lift off the bottom of the page as early as 1440 with Gutenberg's invention of movable type for printing. That single advance was momentous – at last ideas could be exchanged freely without regard to distance or to time – but it was virtually the only communications advance that would be made until the middle of the nineteenth century, some four hundred years later.

But look what has happened since. Electrical power, telephones, the invention of powered flight, motion picture film, radio, television, computers – all of these are now so much a part of our society we tend to forget how much they change the way we live and how much they change us.

For example, there's no doubt that television has made us into a visually sophisticated audience. The nightly bombardment of artfully contrived graphic images in the commercials, along with the beautifully shot and edited sequences in the dramas and documentaries we see educate us all in the basics of picture composition, whether we know it or not. Similarly, almost all of us, even very young children, are now so highly trained that extremely rapid sequences of sounds and pictures can be correctly interpreted, their messages received and understood, in just thirty seconds – the average duration of the TV commercial.

Television is now such a powerful and all-pervasive medium the mere sight of a TV camera can apparently persuade people to say and do things they'd never dream of in 'real life'. Walk up to a perfect stranger, ask 'How's your sex life?' and be prepared for a smack in the nose. But do the same thing accompanied by a full TV crew and your stranger is quite likely to grin weakly, then proceed to give a fairly detailed reply, possibly accompanied with photographs in extreme cases.

But if television has changed the way we act and heightened our capacity to receive and translate visual images, the computer is in the process of changing the way we think. The dull plastic boxes topped with screens many of us now have sitting on our desks are capable of working extremely quickly – if you call work the ability to use data to solve problems – and we are being compelled to catch up. This is largely a matter of marketing – it's essential for us all to want the newest car, the lastest fashions, the fastest computer, because if we didn't our economy would collapse. But when you trade in your old computer for a new, much, *much* faster model you'd be forgiven for feeling just a trifle peeved at the yawning chasm between its operating speed and yours – whether you could use all that extra speed or not.

These words are being written on what, in computer terms, is virtually a steam-powered machine – an eight-year-old PC-XT. Compared with today's machines it's mind-bendingly slow, phenomenally underfeatured and aesthetically monstrous. Yet it does the job I want it to do perfectly well working at a comfortable speed – which is still somewhat faster than mine – and having got used to its little idiosyncrasies I see no reason to change it. Eight years ago I felt very avant-garde when I bought it; today, even though it's laughably out-dated, it remains an ideal machine for the job.

For me – and I suspect for many others – new technology has no automatic right to be considered superior to old, and the same must be said for some of the new fads and fashions coming on to the conference scene. Before irrevocably casting myself as an electronic Luddite, however, I hasten to add that some of these new technologies have had a wonderfully invigorating effect on traditional conference practices, allowing people to communicate effectively using totally novel and sometimes very exciting techniques.

The growth of the new technologies has affected the conference market in two ways: presentations at conventional conferences and events may be enhanced by equipment which uses new technology; or the technology may itself lead to the creation of a new method of conference communication. Some advances – the increasing use of computers for instance – have an effect right across the market so it's pointless to categorise technologies by their applications – there are so many.

LASERS

An expensive light beam to some, for others, a facility that can produce the most stunning lighting effects, lasers have come a long way since those flickering beams circled aimlessly over pop fans at concerts in the 1960s. Used with some discretion lasers can inject an exciting visual note into any event that's going for sensation; it may be a visual cliché but the company logo lasered on to a suitably grand surface at a climactic moment can still bring a lump to the throat – and a pain to the wallet, because laser equipment isn't cheap.

On a much smaller scale the laser pointer, a small, hand-held device to help presenters draw attention to parts of a large screen or blackboard display, is a good example of new technology providing clear benefits over the conventional alternatives. Long wooden or plastic pointers are usually difficult for the audience to see, devices using conventional light beams suffer similar disadvantages in bright light, but the hand-held laser pointer delivers a bright spot of red light which attracts the audience's attention even when used up to 150 feet away from the screen and in bright light. In darkness the laser pointer has a range of nearly half a mile!

SLIDE PROJECTORS

Although basically still a device to shine a bright lamp through a 35mm slide, the slide projector has been improved and refined until today it's far more reliable, powerful – and even somewhat faster – than its ancestors. What gives it a place in a discussion on new technology, however, is its use with computers. A number of modern slide projectors, controlled by computer with a sound track mastered on digital audio-tape and played through state-of-the-art loudspeakers can create a range of stunning effects, particularly when a multi-screen format is used. The computer is perfect for this kind of task; it easily copes with the hundreds of instructions that must be issued to the projectors, it repeats them reliably and has enough spare capacity to handle the operation of other equipment, such as lights and video projectors. I have even heard rumours of a computer program that asks for basic information on a subject then writes an audio-visual script. I can only hope these rumours are false.

COMPUTERS AND CD-ROM

CD-ROM (CD for compact disc, ROM for read-only memory, indicating that the disc is for replaying, not recording) gives today's powerful computers a medium that opens up wonderful possibilities for conference and event planners. With computer memories growing ever larger and operating speeds increasing at a phenomenal rate, the devices which store computer instructions and information – tape in the early days, then 360 Kb floppy disks, now the 3.5in high density disks and giant capacity hard disks – have always seemed to lag behind the computer's capacity to handle information. Now, fitted with a CD-ROM drive, even the most powerful business computer has met its match.

Looking exactly like the compact disc that plays music on a sound system, the computer CD slots into a unit in the computer, just as a conventional computer disk – but it's capable of storing a vast amount of data. Computer technology is progressing in leaps and bounds, so it's asking for trouble to quote figures, but at the time of writing there are CD-ROM units available which can store as much as 150,000 pages of text – you'd need 480 conventional computer disks to hold that amount. Although CD-ROM is supposed to be a 'read-only' medium, a new format – CD-ROM/XA – is recordable, accepting sound and pictures as well as text. Access to all this data is blindingly fast – around 280 milliseconds (ms) – and it's this speed of access coupled with the modern computer's fast processing speeds that makes the arrival of CD-ROM such an exciting development.

The new medium can store enough data to enable a computer to display on its screen moving pictures in colour. As this consumes enormous quantities of disk space and requires a great deal of computer memory only relatively short sequences have been seen to date; but, as I said earlier, in the computer market advances are being made so rapidly that by the time this is in print these disadvantages will probably have been overcome.

But putting movies on to a computer screen is only one benefit brought by compact discs. Although 'real-life' motion pictures use a great amount of disk storage space and only short sequences are possible, animated graphics use far less so it's possible to replay much lengthier graphic sequences, which can look extremely impressive when used either to support a spoken presentation or as attractive display pieces in their own right. And, if a sound track is required, the compact disc can also store the necessary information to replay music, sound effects and voices, with separate tracks assigned to carry alternative language versions if desired. The tiny loudspeakers found inside most computers don't do justice to the sound quality it's possible to obtain from this medium, but computer manufacturers are already beginning to address this deficiency – and for group presentation purposes the signal would almost certainly be fed to a separate amplifier and loudspeakers to obtain the best quality.

As well as its awesome storage capacity CD-ROM offers one

more feature that can offer a benefit to conference planners – it can provide access to random pieces of information extremely quickly. I mentioned in Chapter 7 that one area in which this ability could be put to good use was the AGM, where at one large company's meeting the platform speakers were supplied with television screens, connected to a backstage replay unit. As members of the audience requested information or asked questions, backstage operators cued in relevant sections from the disk, giving platform speakers a screen full of information which let them respond quickly, whatever the subject. The meeting I had in mind took place around four years ago and the unit replayed video disks, large, relatively expensive to produce and lacking the storage capacity of CD-ROM. Today, one well-specified standard office PC fitted with a CD-ROM drive would be capable of doing the same job just as effectively – and, with CD-ROMs holding the equivalent of around half the *Encyclopaedia Britannica*, with storage capacity to spare.

One multinational company recently delivered an entire overseas presentation using CD-ROM. Short, 'live action' sequences on 1in videotape were cut into 'windows' in the screen area, graphic frames and sequences were edited together from a variety of sources and a music, effects and voice track added. Everything was then mastered on to CD-ROM – and an executive of the company flew to Spain with one small CD in his briefcase. At the conference venue a video projection unit and sound system were connected to a PC, the disk inserted – and the executive sat at the computer keyboard tapping the spacebar to cue each part of the presentation.

The computer equipment needed to make use of CD-ROM technology is not vastly expensive. For the most spectacular results the medium demands a great deal of computer memory, but many companies have already invested in PCs with sufficient memory to cope, and in any case extra memory is inexpensive and easily installed. CD-ROM units cost less than two hundred pounds now and are likely to become even cheaper. Where extra expense would be required is in the design of a CD-ROM presentation and, in the mastering, the making of the disk itself. Both these operations require specialised skills and mastering also requires special equipment, but in this exciting new field there are a growing number of companies able to provide these services.

Incidentally, although the mastering process can be fairly expensive (I won't quote prices – they go out of date very quickly!) the run-on cost for pressing more copies of a CD-ROM is very low. One company recently took advantage of this by mailing copies of its fact-filled CD-ROM to many of its customers – who must have been greatly impressed with the company's use of the latest communications technology.

THE VIDEOPHONE

We've been joking about them for years, but at last they've arrived. Small screens and jerky pictures won't do their image – or yours – much good at the moment, but like every other piece of new technology mentioned here, the videophone is bound to get better – not to mention smaller, cheaper and more user-friendly.

In its current guise it's little more than a gimmick. The 3in screen *is* minuscule, the picture is transmitted in chunks refreshed every few seconds so an unnerving jerkiness is unavoidable, and if you want to hold an eyeball-to-eyeball conversation with someone outside the UK you'll be out of luck, for the current UK videophone is incompatible with anyone else's; you can talk to your overseas colleague, but the screens will remain blank.

What's interesting about the videophone is the fact that it's here. The technology that makes it possible has been around for some time, but only now is it robust and reliable enough to enter the mass market. Could increasing business use of the videophone affect the conference market? It remains to be seen but I think it's unlikely. The phone – tele or video – is primarily a one-to-one communication medium and if (or when) the multiway videophone comes along it probably won't be able to handle a spirited discussion between a sizeable group of people. The technology that makes the videophone possible, however, not only will have an effect, but it is having an effect as an increasing number of businesspeople take part in teleconferences.

TELECONFERENCING

There have been huge advances in communication technology over the past few years. Pick up the phone and talk to someone in America, and the voice you hear is quite likely to be as clear and lifelike as if it were coming from the next room. And not only have calls to destinations on the other side of the world become clearer, they're also easier and cheaper to make, benefits brought about by new switching techniques and the use of fibre-optic cables and satellites. The technology to transmit and receive pictures as well as sound over long distances has been with us for some considerable time – since 1886 if you believe the claim that German inventor Nipkov got there forty years before Baird – but only during the last few years has business got around to the notion that holding meetings on television could be a good thing. Looking at some of the early teleconferences it's easy to understand why the business world didn't exactly rush into the medium – when it began, teleconferencing suffered from all the worst features of the videophone but on a hideously larger scale.

That it survived is not only a tribute to the engineers who made it so much better, but also because it's a medium that fulfils a very real need. Jetting a group of people around the world to meet another group who've just jetted in from somewhere else can be a fearsomely expensive operation. The travel costs, plus the venue hire, plus the delegates' time, plus the productivity loss because they're not at their office desks adds up to a sizeable sum – which a well-organised teleconference can cut dramatically.

The theory is simple: a group in, say, London gathers in a television studio. This may, in fact, be the company's boardroom in which TV cameras and suitable lighting have been installed, or the group may have travelled to a purpose-built teleconferencing studio nearby. In Rome the group's opposite numbers gather in a similar location and at a set time the lines carrying sound and vision signals between the two locations are switched on. The meeting then proceeds in the normal way, the cameras covering the contributions and reactions of both groups.

Teleconferencing works best with smaller groups or groups who can restrict themselves to fairly well-defined meeting structures. Technical crews have to cover the event 'on the fly' – there's very little chance to rehearse – so a room full of people all trying to speak at once is their idea of hell. In these circumstances, even with a multi-camera set up it's difficult for the technical director to know where to point the cameras; and if the same conditions prevail at the other end of the line, everyone concerned would be better off switching to another channel and settling down to watch the afternoon film.

To give a teleconference the best chance of success, two chairpersons should be appointed, one at each location. If at all possible, the chairpersons should work out an agenda which should be circulated to all concerned – especially the technical crew – at least a few days before the conference itself. The chairpersons should also liaise with their respective technicians in advance, giving them a broad indication of the way they see the conference proceeding and allocating priority to certain subjects or speakers. There's a tricky balance to be struck between effectiveness and spontaneity – the conference has objectives to achieve so a certain amount of pre-planning is advisable; but at the same time everyone should feel free to contribute if they wish.

It's interesting to note that broadcast television stopped being 'live' many years ago partly because producers said they could get a much more natural effect by recording programmes in unnatural bits and pieces instead of shooting them 'as they happened'. There's no doubt the television camera modifies people's behaviour and its unreasonable to expect the same degree of rapport between groups viewing each other on television screens as you might expect if they were facing each other across a conference table. Although the technical problems of teleconferencing have largely been overcome there remains a human problem – how to get groups of ordinary people to relax and react naturally when faced with TV cameras and lights. Some executives have a natural talent for expressing themselves on camera, some have gained it by attending a relevant course and for these people teleconferencing will seem a relatively natural medium. Others may find it awkward to handle and before taking the plunge the in-house organiser might find it worthwhile arranging a dry run with everyone concerned, using cameras and lights if possible, and mocking up the overseas team's contribution.

But using television to link two locations is a technique that can do more than just allow people to talk to each other. The teleconference is like a television show that can do whatever the client wants. Cameras can be arranged to show not just the speakers, but also the subject of the conference, so company engineers might show components to overseas colleagues to help overcome technical problems; scientists could share information in the form of graphs or models; designers in one country could stage a fashion show for buyers in another – and so on. And the television link can also be used to bring to a conference a speaker who might otherwise have been absent – an expert who is out of the country or a personality who can't attend in person, for example.

Budget is, of course, a major factor when considering teleconferencing, but the next major application forecast to hit the business communication process is aimed at reducing costs. Some video conference systems take up dedicated space in office complexes, use satellites and cost many thousands of pounds per site. But smaller, near portable versions of these 'whole room' systems are available. The so-called 'peer to peer' system can be set up in a conference room and hooked up via dedicated lines. A camera and video viewer can allow two or three people at a time to communicate down the hall or across the world, providing a portable system that costs just a few thousand pounds and can be used for many other purposes. At the time of writing there are two of these systems available in America and more advances are promised to help reduce costs still further. New signal compression techniques such as ISDN and ISDN2, along with advances in fibre-optic cables, are now enabling desktop PCs to 'talk' to each other through telephone lines, sending not only data but also moving pictures, graphics and sounds. With a small video camera mounted on top of a computer monitor at each end, two people sitting at their desks separated by thousands of miles can hold a conference almost as easily and productively as if they were sitting face to face. And to arrange a teleconference involving perhaps six people at each end it's only necessary to add two or three cameras, plan a seating layout – with microphones built into a conference desk, perhaps – and to arrange for a separate camera to show three dimensional objects in detail if necessary. Teleconferencing systems like these are working now and, at a time when many companies are looking for new ways to reduce costs or are expanding into overseas markets, they are becoming increasingly popular.

On the face of it, teleconferencing has everything it takes to put an end to traditional meetings. It saves time and travel, it saves money – and the thought of the fixed-duration teleconference booking must concentrate the executive mind wonderfully. But there are some things a 'live' conference can do that can't be measured so easily. There are contacts to be made, new places to visit, the cut and thrust of heated argument to be experienced at first hand – and while these remain important, although teleconferencing will remain a valuable addition to the conference organiser's armoury, it will be no substitute for the real thing.

INTERACTIVE VIDEO

Used mainly in training and point-of-sale situations, interactive video may also have a conference use in exhibitions or as an information point at AGMs. The term describes a video programme – once played from tape but now almost always from video disk or CD-ROM – that responds to commands or requests from viewers. In the point-of-sale context this might be a programme located in a store, giving customers the opportunity of 'asking' questions on a new product or service by listing a menu of choice on screen. In training, the programme takes students through a series of questions, reacting to their responses either by progressing the lesson or returning to incorrectly answered questions.

As mentioned before, the video disk has provided AGM platform speakers with instant screen information on a wide variety of topics relevant to the company and its shareholders. Video disks have also been used in interactive video units at AGMs. Placed in attractive and eye-catching cabinets in the reception areas, an 'attractor' sound and vision sequence invited shareholders to ask about the company – a nice touch and one that many shareholders appreciated.

Interactivity, a new concept only a comparatively short time ago, is now commonplace. Tap an instruction on to a computer keyboard and the machine responds. And it's the computer which can now produce interactive programmes for conference presentations, point-of-sale and training, with CD-ROMs which offer all the benefits of video disk at far less cost.

HOLOGRAPHY

In the novel *Fahrenheit 451* by Ray Bradbury there is a sequence describing the television room of the future. The room is bare, an empty shell – until holograms are projected into it and it becomes peopled with three-dimensional figures, actors and actresses who invite viewers to join them in the room as they play out a drama or act out a comedy – and to respond to their projected images as if the images were real.

Whether you find the idea fascinating or frightening it's now edging out of fantasy and into reality. Holographic images have been projected and although they're still too small to be of much use in the conference field, imagine the effect on the teleconferencing market if, one day, life-size, three-dimensional speaking images could be piped around the world. You read it here first!

COMPUTER-GENERATED GRAPHICS

The organiser setting out to produce graphic images for an event – whether they're simple 'one-off' slides or complex animated sequences – has to achieve a high standard. As I said earlier, broadcast TV saturates us with high quality images and we now expect the same quality whenever we see graphics on a TV screen.

It was once difficult and expensive to produce graphics to

broadcast standards; costly equipment and scarce skills were all in the hands of the major broadcasting organisations or the bigger video facility or production houses and most conference organisers had to face the stark choice of either paying up or doing without.

Enter – once again – the computer. Software packages are now available to enable anyone with a reasonably powerful PC to create a range of lettered slides, charts and diagrams, and even animated sequences. The computer lets the operator create the image, position it, rotate it, increase or decrease its size and many other operations until it's precisely what is wanted. The operator then 'saves' the image on to a computer disk for recalling later to produce the slide or for changing the image if it's necessary.

Most graphics produced in-house in this way utilise software employing the '1,000-line system' which gives high-resolution images. The '1,000 lines' refers to the approximate number of pixels or picture cells across the top of the screen – a normal TV screen has 990 pixels across the top and 660 down the side giving 650,000 in all, easily sufficient to produce good quality images with reasonable resolution – though not as good as 4,000-line systems which offer superb resolution but at a much higher price.

VIDEO GRAPHICS

Aside from the extremely wide range of visual effects possible in the video editing suite, a computerised portable video titling and effects unit can be used to produce a wide range of video graphics, not only before the event takes place, but also on the day itself. If a slide is discovered to be wrong it's difficult to change it – if the image is on video, however, it's a fairly easy matter to run it through the computer and put it right – even within minutes of the start.

SUMMARY

The computer seems to have made fairly frequent appearances in this chapter and there are still some computer operations we haven't mentioned; desk-top publishing for example which, although not directly related to conferences, certainly has a major role to play in the associated promotional and PR activities. Then there's outlining, a unique facility the computer offers writers and organisers, enabling them to construct plans in the most flexible, natural way. I said earlier that the computer can change the way we think and an outlining software package certainly shows how to approach the business of planning – a script, a meeting, a big event – logically, clearly and thoroughly. Everything discussed here has been to do with machines, equipment and electronics. But, conferences, events and seminars are, of course, to do with people and, however wonderful, amazing or just plain awe-inspiring your technical support, it's the human element that makes the difference between success and failure. There may be some events in which flashy graphics, loud music and disembodied voices successfully pummel an audience into submission, but as a general rule the events audiences remember are the ones in which they feel they've been involved, in which the people on the platform or at the lectern spoke to them, in which they were motivated by men and women, not by machinery.

The ideal conference would consist of one person standing in front of a plain backdrop holding an audience spellbound for an hour or so. Not many people can do that, so we have to give lesser mortals a little support – and support is what every piece of technology discussed here ought to do. When the equipment is the star of the show, beware! Either the message has been forgotten by the show's planners or there never was a message.

And one last word on technology. Everything in this chapter is already out of date and all predictions made are hopelessly conservative. For although the advances we've seen in the last few years have been quite amazing, I think it's as well to remember the immortal words of Al Jolson as he announced some interesting new technology back in 1927: 'You ain't heard nothin' yet!'

11 EVALUATING THE EVENT

● After the event ● How much has it cost? ● Money well spent? ● Did it work? ● The lessons ● The cost-effective event ● Summary

There once was a time – it is alleged – when many events took place with little regard to cost; when companies seemed to feel it was a good idea to send selected executives and staff to stay in three-star hotels where they would be exposed to expensive presentations rich in creativity but somewhat short on clarity; when the company conference was widely regarded as an appropriate occasion for everyone to have a good time.

If ever this was true, it certainly isn't now. 'Was it worth it?' is the question that is – or should be – asked after every major event in today's economic climate and it's a question every organiser should be ready to answer.

But 'Was it worth it?' is a question that can't always be answered in strictly financial terms, at least not in the short run. So, in attempting to evaluate the effectiveness of an event, perhaps we should begin by asking 'Did it work?' – in other words, did it fulfil the aims and achieve the objectives set for it? Leaving aside events designed specifically to make money, profit is a word that probably didn't appear often, if at all, in your original planning documents; but when it's all over and you're counting the cost, it's reasonable to try to discover what's been gained for the money spent.

AFTER THE EVENT

You might start by listing the component parts of the event and commenting on their quality. Done in the cold, grey light of day some time after the event this can be a most instructive process, for now you'll be able to isolate each event element, make an honest judgement on its value to the event as a whole and suggest how that value could have been increased. I show the bare bones of such a checklist on pages 170–1; again, your checklist may be different depending upon the nature and style of your event.

HOW MUCH HAS IT COST?

But how much has really been spent? Some costs are easily quantifiable: the venue hire, accommodation, production costs and so on. Others may be hidden, but they also have to be taken into account if the true cost of an event is to be found. How many hours have your in-house production team spent on the event, for example? The company people who spoke at the event no doubt spent time preparing scripts and support materials – or briefing others to do some of the work for them. And all company personnel involved in the event presumably weren't able to do their normal work on the day it occurred – perhaps even for some time before and after. All these things add to costs, but if you're being really ruthless about the cost-effectiveness of events you organise for your company, they should be taken into account. To be scientific about it, you might consider the formula:

$$\frac{C + T + A + P}{D} = CD$$

Where C = the Cost of the contributions made by every participant in the event; T = Travel expenses; A = Accommodation, including food and drink; P = Production costs, including the cost of the venue, equipment hire, support material such as slides, video etc. Divide that sum by D = the number of Delegates attending the event – and you have an approximate CD, or Cost per Delegate.

It's 'C' – the cost of contributions made by participants – where underestimating is all too easy. Executives speaking at a one-day event may spend perhaps another day of their time travelling to and from the venue, and before that they might have spent a further half-day preparing their material. Also, while away at the conference they are not doing their normal work – which means someone else is having to do it or it isn't being done; either way, it's extra expense. It also has to be said that at one time the company conference frequently presented an opportunity to eat, drink and be merry at the company's expense – and, also at the company's expense, to suffer for it over the ensuing day or two. As the economy has become tougher those opportunities have vanished.

MONEY WELL SPENT?

Having found out how much you've spent on each delegate you can begin to discover whether it was money well spent. The effect of an event aimed at improving the performance of a group of people is relatively easy to evaluate; after the conference did they sell more cars, produce more widgets or deal with more customers? If they did – everything else being equal – then the extra profit your company makes could be attributed to the conference.

But, what if the event's objective is to improve morale, smooth the path for organisational changes, or inform or train company staff? These are all important and valuable aims, but none is likely to show immediate profit in financial terms. In these instances it's best to look upon the event as a very necessary part of a staff communications programme and an investment in the company's future, and to squeeze from it every ounce of value possible. This is almost certain to pay off in the long run, even in financial terms. The alternative is to cancel – and to accept the inevitable consequences of falling morale, inability to accept change and lower productivity.

DID IT WORK?

Whether you can measure the event's effectiveness in financial terms or not, it will still be extremely useful to find out how the

THE EVENT OBJECTIVE

(At the head of the checklist write a short description of the objective the event set out to achieve. Keep it in mind when completing the document.)

PRINT

Were you happy with the design and layout? Was the content correct? Was it effective/well written? Was the print material delivered on time? Quote compared with cost?

VENUE

Was it in the right location? Was it the right size? Ratings for accommodation/food/service? Were the facilities suitable? Were the staff helpful? Delegates' comments? Quote compared with cost?

TRANSPORT

Were the vehicles in good condition? Were they punctual? Was the transport organisation efficient? Were the drivers polite and helpful? Quote compared with cost?

DESIGN

Ratings for the appearance of signage/the set/lighting/venue dressing? Were the design elements delivered/installed on time? Did delegates comment on any design aspects? Quote compared with cost?

TECHNICAL FACILITIES

How well did your supplier perform? Were the equipment installers/operators efficient? Were there any equipment malfunctions? Causes? Quote compared with cost?

SPEAKERS

Was the script effective? Was the style suitable? Was the content clear? How was the material delivered? Did support equipment and material work? Speakers' assessments of their performance? Your assessment? Delegates' comments? Scriptwriter: comprehension, speed, punctuality? Quote compared with cost?

PRESENTATION

Was the style suitable? Was the design/music/venue right for this event? Was the event long enough/too short/too long? Delegates' comments? Quote compared with cost?

DELEGATES' COMMENTS

Any comments either not covered by the above or not directly concerned with this event, but which may be useful when planning another.

CLIENT'S COMMENTS

What was liked about the event? What wasn't liked? Was the brief carried out? Have there been any management/staff reactions? Are results measurable? If so, what has been achieved? Quote compared with cost. And was the cost worth it?

delegates reacted to it – indeed, the checklist outlined on page 170 depends upon some straight answers from your audience. What worked and what didn't? Which points came across well and which were lost? A few 'off the cuff' responses might be obtained by mingling with the audience after the event, armed with either a good memory or a cassette recorder. But although these instant reactions will be valuable, they'll inevitably be coloured by the atmosphere surrounding the event; to gain a much clearer idea of the lasting impressions gained by members of the audience, ask some of them to complete a questionnaire a few days after the event. Make it simple – a 'tick the relevant box' approach is ideal – and put in a few questions designed to test whether the main conference messages were received and understood.

In addition to those 'message' questions, the questionnaire should attempt to discover the audience's views on:

- **The venue**   Was it in the right location, was it easy to reach with adequate car parking, was it comfortable, was the service and catering good, were the venue staff efficient?

- **The organisation**   Were you aware of the event before it occurred, were travel arrangements made efficiently, were seating arrangements satisfactory, were support materials – agendas, voting papers, information sheets etc. – well prepared?

- **The event**   Was it well produced, could it be seen and heard clearly, were the speakers effective, was the support material – video, AV etc. – good, was there enough time for questions, did you feel involved, what did you learn?

- **The follow-up**   Has there been an official follow-up, if not, should there be, what was the immediate result of the event, are further actions planned?

Devising a questionnaire like this is best done during the early planning stages when the aims and objectives of the event are clearly defined for the first time. Deeper into the project it's just possible your clear vision may become a tiny bit blurred – and in any case there'll be a great number of other, far more important things to do!

Getting people to complete a questionnaire can be difficult, particularly in the days following an event when everyone is busy catching up with work. Ways around this problem include: making the questionnaire really easy to complete; a personal visit armed with cassette recorder; a questionnaire competition with prizes; and constant nagging. The last is not recommended but is sadly often necessary.

THE LESSONS

A questionnaire like the one above and the checklist mentioned earlier not only make you wise after the event: more important, they make you wise before the next one. If you're organising and producing the next event using in-house resources, analysis of these documents will tell you a great deal about what you should do and what to avoid. If an outside agency has just produced an event for you, ask if they will undertake some form of evaluation procedure, a request they'll probably be happy to grant. Most conference production companies know that corporate clients are putting more and more emphasis on effective conference communication, and less and less on superficial glitz and glamour, so they'll be as anxious as you are to ensure that all the conference messages have gone home effectively.

And who should see the results of this research? The people who paid for the event – your fellow directors or superiors perhaps – should certainly be given a report on how effective it was, what it lacked and what could improve it next time around. An honest, well-presented research document – ideally with some ad-lib comments from the respondents to help bring it to life – shows everyone that you know the vital importance of making the event work.

And the participants too need to know how they performed. Addressing audiences at company conferences – particularly the larger events – can be an uncomfortable experience for some, so it's good for them to know if they've done well; and if they haven't, for them to discover just what went wrong, along with some helpful (and confidential) advice on how to get it right next time.

And don't forget the technical crew. If the event went well

their contribution was a major factor and, if technical foul-ups spoiled it, they certainly need to know.

THE COST-EFFECTIVE EVENT

Evaluating the event that's just ended should help to make your next event even more effective at even less cost. But in case you have had to skip the evaluation stage, or are organising or producing a conference for the first time, here are just a few ways to help you get the best value for your conference money.

- Keep the event short. If possible book half a day instead of a full day, so only one night's accommodation is necessary.

- Get maximum value for the event by packing more in. Have a running buffet instead of lunches, make more use of 'break-out' sessions to get maximum involvement from delegates, and use evening as well as daytime sessions.

- Take extra care choosing venues. Venue technical facilities are improving and venues with good facilities could be better value – you'll save the cost of equipment hire.

- Be ruthless with delegate lists. Restrict delegates to those most likely to benefit. Smaller numbers could mean a smaller venue with savings in venue, accommodation and catering costs.

- If you're using outside suppliers to produce your event, shop around; some are offering special, low-price conference packages consisting of ready-made sets and a selection of standard equipment.

- If you are consistently pleased with an outside supplier's work, consider a long-term arrangement with them; the guarantee of regular work should result in a reduction in their charges.

- Haggle. There are good bargains to be had in all sectors of the conference market so don't accept the first reduction you're offered; set your own price and see how close you can get to it.

Summary

In the last two or three years there has been plenty of change in the conference industry. As the economic climate has become tougher, so a great many extras have been trimmed from corporate events. Exotic locations are now rarely specified, formats have become much simplified, spectacular audio-visual or video modules are no longer produced. The company event today is likely to be tighter, leaner, more purposeful – and much more a creation of the client than the professional conference production house.

This is as it should be, as even the professionals would admit. In fact, for many years the professionals have been actively trying to persuade their clients to become more closely involved in the production process and achieve a greater understanding of the conference medium. It's happened, and what we see now is a far more equitable balance being struck between the people who specify and pay for the work, and the people who carry it out. The professionals who once created colourful theatrical occasions for their clients now tend to produce hard-working, down-to-earth events which offer real value for money; while at the same time clients are now far more experienced in conference technicalities and are becoming more and more involved in conference production – up to and including the creation of complete events using in-house resources.

The next few years should see the conference medium undergo even more radical changes as the new communications technologies become more widely established. Video conferencing has been around for some years, always on the verge of revolutionising the conference market, yet never quite seeming to do so. But the technology is developing rapidly, prices are falling, common worldwide standards are being established and an increasing number of medium to large-sized companies are dipping a toe into the teleconferencing pond. For example, one of the UK's three national power-generating companies has equipped its sites in England and Wales with teleconferencing systems, allowing staff to have instant face-to-face meetings with colleagues all over the UK. The system also allows users to exchange documents or show live action from a remote camera –

and it costs £800,000. But costs are already tumbling. The equipment to set up two teleconference rooms allowing two groups, each of around six people, to hold a conference now costs around £70,000 – although to make the Teleconference Room aesthetically pleasing would add a fair amount to that sum. Whether teleconferencing will replace conventional face-to-face meetings remains to be seen. There's no doubt that it's a very useful addition to a company's communications strategy.

The computer as a low-cost graphics generator offers enormous advantages to conference organisers, while at the same time posing the very real danger that in inexperienced hands the material it creates may turn events into fast-moving graphic nightmares. Armed with a powerful modern computer and some of the latest software, almost anyone can create a complete range of conference support material – though whether it will be pleasant to look at, readable or effective is another matter. The temptation to use this enormously powerful and versatile tool is great, but it should be resisted if possible unless or until some experience in basic design rules has been gained.

In a medium that depends so much upon the interchange of words and human expressions, technology must always play second fiddle. It should be there to support a message, never to supplant it – and when the balance is right, planning and organising an event which combines well-rehearsed, persuasive speakers, backed by powerful yet restrained technical support, can be a truly satisfying experience for all concerned – producer, participants and the most important group of people in the conference world, the audience.

DIRECTORY OF SUPPLIERS

N.B. On 16 April 1995, national dialling codes will change to include a '1' after the initial '0'. For example, London codes will change to 0171 and 0181. The exceptions to this are Bristol, Leeds, Leicester, Nottingham and Sheffield. For further information call 0800 01 01 01.

Venues

Do you intend to find your own venue – or are you going to leave the task to a specialist company? Whichever path you choose there are plenty of organisations waiting to help you, from hotels and local authorities to venue finding companies specialising in making the perfect match between client and venue. And don't forget, help in finding a venue is almost always free; hotels and conference centres want your business and they'll pay the venue-finder's costs.

The list below is not intended to be exhaustive but to give some small indication of the range and location of conference venues.

ABERDEEN

Exhibition & Conference Centre
Bridge of Don
Aberdeen AB23 8BL
TEL: 0224 824824

Aberdeen Music Hall
Union Street
Aberdeen AB1 1QS
TEL: 0224 632080

ALDEBURGH

Snape Maltings Concert Hall
Aldeburgh Foundation
Aldeburgh
Suffolk 1P15 5AX
TEL: 0728 452935

ALDERSHOT

West End Centre
Queens Road
Aldershot
Hants GU11 3JD
TEL: 0252 21158

ARUNDEL

Amberley Castle
Amberley
Nr Arundel
W. Sussex BN18 9ND
TEL: 0798 831992

ASHFORD

Ashford International Hotel
Simone Weil Avenue
Ashford
Kent TN24 8UX
TEL: 0233 611444

AVIEMORE

Aviemore Centre
Aviemore
Invernesshire PH22 1PF
TEL: 0479 810624

AYLESBURY

Aylesbury Forte Crest Hotel
Aston Clinton Road
Aylesbury
Bucks HP22 5AA
TEL: 0296 393388

BARROW-IN-FURNESS

Forum 28
28 Duke Street
Barrow-in-Furness
Cumbria LA14 1HU
TEL: 0229 820000

BASINGSTOKE

Central Studio
Queen Mary's College
Cliddesden Road
Basingstoke
Hants RG21 3HF
TEL: 0256 479221

BATH

Theatre Royal
Sawclose
Bath
Avon BA1 1ET
TEL: 0225 448815

BEDFORD

Silsoe Campus
Silsoe
Beds MK45 4DT
TEL: 0525 860428

St Pauls Centre
St Pauls Square
Beds MK40 1SJ
TEL: 0234 344813

BELFAST

Ulster Hall
Bedford Street
Belfast BT2 7FF
TEL: 0232 323900

BEXHILL-ON-SEA

De La Warr Pavilion
The Marina
Bexhill-on-Sea
E. Sussex TN40 1DP
TEL: 0424 212023

BIRMINGHAM

Birmingham Conservatoire
Paradise Place
Birmingham B3 3HG
TEL: 021–235 5909

*Birmingham Marketing
Partnership*
9 The Wharf
Bridge Street
Birmingham B1 2JS
TEL: 021–631 2401

Birmingham Symphony Hall
Convention Centre
Broad Street
Birmingham B1 2EA
TEL: 021–200 2000

*British Association of
Conference Towns*
First Floor, Elizabeth House
22 Suffolk Street
Queensway
Birmingham B1 1LS
TEL: 021–616 1400

The Crescent Theatre
Cumberland Street
Brindley Place
Birmingham B1 2JA
TEL: 021–643 5859

James Gracie Conference Centre
38 Wake Green Road
Moseley
Birmingham B13 9PE
TEL: 021–449 4137

Lucas House Conference Centre
48 Edgbaston Park Road
Birmingham B15 2RA
TEL: 021–455 0921

Metropole Hotel
National Exhibition Centre
Birmingham B40 1PP
TEL: 021–780 4242

National Exhibition Centre
Birmingham B40 1NT
TEL: 021–780 4141

BLACKBURN

King George's Hall
Northgate
Blackburn
Lancs BB2 1AA
TEL: 0254 582579

BLACKPOOL

Winter Gardens & Opera House
91 Church Street
Blackpool
Lancs FY1 1HW
TEL: 0253 25252

BLANDFORD

Bryanston Arts Centre
Blandford
Dorset DT11 0PX
TEL: 0258 456533

BOGNOR REGIS

Bognor Regis Centre
Belmont Street
Bognor Regis
W. Sussex PO21 1BL
TEL: 0243 865915

BOLTON

Albert Halls
Victoria Square
Town Hall
Bolton
Lancs BL1 4TG
TEL: 0204 22311

BOURNEMOUTH

Bournemouth International Centre
Exeter Road
Bournemouth
Dorset BH2 5BH
TEL: 0202 552122

BRADFORD

McMillan Hall of Residence
Easby Road
Bradford BD7 1QZ
TEL: 0274 733291

St Georges Concert Hall
Bridge Street
Bradford
W. Yorks BD1 1JS
TEL: 0274 752186

BRENTFORD

Fountain Leisure Centre
658 Chiswick High Road
Brentford
Middx TW8 0HJ
TEL: 081–994 6901

Syon Park Conference Centre
Syon Park
Brentford
Middx TW8 8JF
TEL: 081–568 0778

Watermans Art Centre
40 High Street
Brentford
Middx TW8 0DS
TEL: 081–847 5651

BRENTWOOD

The Brentwood Centre
Doddinghurst Road
Brentwood
Essex CM15 4NN
TEL: 0277 215151

BRIGHTON

The Brighton Centre
Kings Road
Brighton
E. Sussex BN1 2GR
TEL: 0273 203131

The Dome Complex
29 New Road
Brighton
E. Sussex BN1 1UG
TEL: 0273 674357

BRISTOL

Bristol Arnolfini
16 Narrow Quay
Bristol BS1 4QA
TEL: 0272 299191

Bristol Old Vic Company
Theatre Royal
King Street
Bristol BS1 4ED
TEL: 0272 277466

Bristol University Conference Centre
The Hawthorns
Woodland Road
Bristol BS8 1UB
TEL: 0272 238028

Bristol University Exhibition Centre
3 Priory Road
Clifton
Bristol BS8 1TX
TEL: 0272 238038

Thornbury Leisure Centre
Alveston Hill
Thornbury
Bristol BS12 2JB
TEL: 0454 417973

Yate Leisure Centre
Kennedy Way
Yate
Bristol BS17 4XE
TEL: 0454 310111

Watershed Media Centre
1 Canons Road
Bristol BS1 5TX
TEL: 0272 272082

CAMBERLEY

Civic Hall
Knoll Road
Camberley
Surrey GU15 3SY
TEL: 0276 26978

CAMBRIDGE

Cambridge Corn Exchange
3 Parsons Court
Wheeler Street
Cambridge CB2 3QE
TEL: 0223 463204

Kelsey Kerridge Sports Hall
Queen Anne Terrace
Cambridge CB1 1NA
TEL: 0223 463210

CANTERBURY

Marlowe Theatre
The Friars
Canterbury
Kent CT1 2AS
TEL: 0227 767246

CARDIFF

Cardiff World Trade Centre
Harlech Court
Off Bute Terrace
Cardiff
South Glamorgan CF1 2FE
TEL: 0222 464141

St Davids Hall
The Hayes
Cardiff
South Glamorgan CF1 2SH
TEL: 0222 342611

CARLISLE

The Sands Centre
The Sands
Carlisle CA1 1JQ
TEL: 0228 810208

CHELTENHAM

Cheltenham Town Hall
Imperial Square
Cheltenham
Glos GL50 1QA
TEL: 0242 573902

The Pittville Pump Room
Town Hall
Imperial Square
Cheltenham
Glos GL50 1QA
TEL: 0242 521621

CHESSINGTON

Chessington World of Adventures
Leatherhead Road
Chessington
Surrey KT9 2NE
TEL: 0372 724720

CHESTERFIELD

The Winding Wheel
13 Holywell Street
Chesterfield
Derbyshire S41 7SA
TEL: 0246 211290

CHIPPING NORTON

Heythrop Park
Chipping Norton
Oxon OX7 5UE
TEL: 0608 677721

COLCHESTER

Colchester Leisure World
Cowdray Avenue
Colchester
Essex CO1 1YH
TEL: 0206 766500

University of Essex Conference Department
Wivenhoe Park
Colchester
Essex CO4 3SQ
TEL: 0206 873333

COVENTRY

Belgrade Theatre
Belgrade Square
Coventry
W. Midlands CV1 1GS
TEL: 0203 256431

Radcliffe House
Conference Department
University of Warwick
Gibbet Hill Road
Coventry
W. Midlands CV4 7AL
TEL: 0203 474711

CRAWLEY

The Hawth Theatre
Hawth Avenue
Crawley
W. Sussex RH10 6YZ
TEL: 0293 552941

CROYDON

Fairfield Halls
Park Lane
Croydon
Surrey CR9 1DG
TEL: 081–681 0821

DARLINGTON

The Arts Centre
Vane Terrace
Darlington
Co Durham DL3 7AX
TEL: 0325 483271

DONCASTER

Doncaster Civic Theatre
Waterdale
Doncaster DN1 3ET
TEL: 0302 322817

DUNDEE

Caird Hall Complex
City Square
Dundee
Scotland DD1 3BD
TEL: 0382 23141

DUNFERMLINE

Carnegie Hall
East Port
Dunfermline
Fife
Scotland KY12 7JE
TEL: 0383 720108

DUNSTABLE

Queensway Hall
Vernon Place
Dunstable
Beds LU5 4EU
TEL: 0582 603326

EASTBOURNE

Congress Theatre
Carlisle Road
Eastbourne
E. Sussex BN21 4BP
TEL: 0323 410048

Devonshire Park Centre
Winter Garden
8 Compton Street
Eastbourne
E. Sussex BN21 4BP
TEL: 0323 415500

EDINBURGH

Royal Highland Centre
Ingliston
Edinburgh EH28 8NF
TEL: 031-333-3036

Usher Hall
Lothian Road
Edinburgh EH1 2EA
TEL: 031–228 1155

EGHAM

Anugraha Hotel
Wick Lane
Englefield Green
Egham
Surrey TW20 0XN
TEL: 0784 434355

ESHER

*Sandown Conference &
Banqueting Centre*
Sandown Park
Portsmouth Road
Esher
Surrey KT10 9AJ
TEL: 0372 467540

EXETER

Beaford Centre
Beaford
Winkleigh
North Devon EX19 8LU
TEL: 08053 201

Northcott Theatre
Stocker Road
Exeter
Devon EX4 4QB
TEL: 0392 56182

The Riverside Leisure Centr
Cowick Street
Exeter
Devon EX4 1AF
TEL: 0392 221771

FARNHAM

Redgrave Theatre
Brightwells
Farnham
Surrey GU9 7SB
TEL: 0252 727000

FOLKESTONE

Leas Cliff Hall
The Leas
Folkestone
Kent CT20 2DZ
TEL: 0303 254695

FROME

Merlin Theatre
Bath Road
Frome
Somerset BA11 2HG
TEL: 0373 461360

GATESHEAD

Metrocentre
Gateshead
Tyne & Wear NE11 9XX
TEL: 091–493 2046

GLASGOW

Kelvin Conference Centre
West of Scotland Science Park
2317 Mary Hill Road
Glasgow G20 0TH
TEL: 041–946 4448

*Scottish Exhibition &
Conference Centre (SECC)*
Finnieston
Glasgow G3 8YW
TEL: 041–248 3000

GLOUCESTER

Guildhall Arts Centre
23 East Gate Street
Glos GL1 1NS
TEL: 0452 505086

GUERNSEY

Beau Sejour Centre
Amherst
St Peter Port
Guernsey GY1 2DL
Chanel Islands
TEL: 0481 727211

GUILDFORD

Guildford Civic Hall
London Road
Guildford
Surrey GU1 2AA
TEL: 0483 444720

*University of Surrey
Conference Office*
Guildford
Surrey GU2 5XH
TEL: 0483 509352

HAYWARDS HEATH

South of England Showground
Ardingly
Haywards Heath
W. Sussex RH17 6TL
TEL: 0444 892700

HARROGATE

Harrogate International Centre
Kings Road
Harrogate
N. Yorks HG1 5LA
TEL: 0423 500500

HEMEL HEMPSTEAD

The Dacorum Pavilion
Marlowes
Hemel Hempstead
Herts HP1 1HA
TEL: 0442 240362

HEREFORD

Hereford Leisure Centre
Holmer Road
Hereford HR4 9UD
TEL: 0432 278178

HULL

Hull City Concert Hall
Victoria Square
Hull
N. Humberside HU1 3NA
TEL: 0482 20123

ISLE OF MAN

Gaiety Theatre
Harris Promenade
Douglas
Isle of Man IM1 2HH
TEL: 0624 625001

JERSEY

Fort Regent Leisure Centre
St Helier
Jersey JE2 4UX
Channel Islands
TEL: 0534 500200

KEELE

*The University of Keele
Conference Centre*
The University of Keele
Keele
Staffs ST5 5BG
TEL: 0782 621111

LEAMINGTON SPA

Royal Spa Centre
Newbold Terrace
Leamington Spa
Warks CV32 4HN
TEL: 0926 334418

LEATHERHEAD

Leatherhead Leisure Centre
Guildford Road
Leatherhead
Surrey KT22 9BL
TEL: 0372 377674

LEEDS

Fairbairn House
71–75 Clarendon Road
Leeds LS2 9RL
TEL: 0532 459034

*Leeds Grand Theatre & Opera
House*
46 New Briggate
Leeds LS1 6NZ
TEL: 0532 456014

LEICESTER

De Montfort Hall
Granville Road
Leics LE1 7RU
TEL: 0533 551502

LINCOLN

North Kesteven Sports Centre
Moor Lane
North Hykeham
Lincoln LN6 9AX
TEL: 0522 685505

LLANDUDNO

Aberconwy Centre
The Promenade
Llandudno
Gwynedd LL30 1BB
TEL: 0492 879771

LONDON

The Bafta Centre
195 Piccadilly
London W1V 9LG
TEL: 071–465 0277

Barbican Centre
Silk Street
Barbican
London EC2Y 8DS
TEL: 071–638 4141

British Tourist Authority
Conference Section
Business Travel Department
Thames Tower
Black's Road
London W6 9EL
TEL: 081–846 9000

City Conference Centre
76 Mark Lane
London EC3R 7JN
TEL: 071–481 8493

Earls Court & Olympia
Limited
Exhibition Centre
Warwick Road
London SW5 9TA
TEL: 071–385 1200

The Hurlingham Club
Ranelagh Gardens
London SW6 3PR
TEL: 071–736 8411

ICA
Nash House
12 Carlton House Terrace
London SW1Y 5AH
TEL: 071–930 0493

London Arena
Limeharbour
Isle of Dogs
London E14 9TH
TEL: 071–538 8880

The Queen Elizabeth II
Conference Centre
Broad Sanctuary
Westminster
London SW1P 3EE
TEL: 071–222 5000

Royal Academy of Arts
Burlington House
Piccadilly
London W1V 0DS
TEL: 071–439 7438

Wembley Conference &
Exhibition Centre
Empire Way
Wembley
Middx HA9 0DW
TEL: 081–902 8833

MAIDSTONE

The Exchange
The Corn Exchange Complex
Earl Street
Maidstone
Kent ME14 1PL
TEL: 0622 602178

MALVERN

Malvern Winter Gardens
Complex
Grange Road
Malvern
Worcs WR14 3HB
TEL: 0684 569256

MANCHESTER

Free Trade Hall
Peter Street
Manchester M2 3NQ
TEL: 061–834 3697

University of Manchester
Conference & Exhibition
Centre
Armitage Centre
Moseley Road
Fallowfield
Manchester M14 6HE
TEL: 061–224 0404

University of Manchester
Conference Office
Oxford Road
Manchester M13 9PL
TEL: 061–275 2155

MARGATE

Winter Gardens
Fort Crescent
Margate
Kent CT9 1HX
TEL: 0843 296111

NEWCASTLE-UPON-TYNE

The Mayfair Suite
Newgate Street
Newcastle-Upon-Tyne
NE1 5XA
TEL: 091–232 3109

NEWPORT

Newport Centre
Kingsway
Newport
Gwent NP9 1UH
TEL: 0633 842154

NEWTON ABBOT

Seale-Hayne Faculty of
Agriculture Conference
Department
University of Plymouth
Newton Abbot
Devon TQ12 6NQ
TEL: 0626 52323

NORTHAMPTON

Derngate Theatre
19–21 Guildhall Road
Northampton NN1 1DP
TEL: 0604 26222

Highgate House Conference
Centre
Creaton
Northampton NN6 8NN
TEL: 060–124 461

NORWICH

St Andrew's & Blackfriars Hall
St Andrews Plain
Norwich
Norfolk NR3 1AU
TEL: 0603 628477

University of East Anglia
Conference Office
University Plain
Norwich NR4 7TJ
TEL: 0603 56161

NOTTINGHAM

*British University
Accommodation Consortium*
PO Box 208
University Park
Nottingham NG7 2RD
TEL: 0602 504571

*East Midlands Conference
Centre*
University Park
Nottingham NG7 2RJ
TEL: 0602 515000

Nottingham Theatre Royal
Royal Centre
Theatre Square
Nottingham NG1 5ND
TEL: 0602 483505

OXFORD

Apollo Leisure (UK) Ltd
PO Box 16
Boars Hill
Oxford OX1 5JB
TEL: 0865 730066

PETERBOROUGH

The Cresset
Rightwell
Bretton Centre
Peterborough
Cambs PE3 8DX
TEL: 0733 265705

PLYMOUTH

Plymouth Pavilions
Millbay Road
Plymouth
Devon PL1 3LF
TEL: 0752 222200

Theatre Royal
Royal Parade
Plymouth
Devon PL1 2TR
TEL: 0752 668282

POOLE

Poole Arts Centre
Kingland Road
Poole
Dorset BH15 1UG
TEL: 0202 670521

PORT TALBOT

Afan Lido Leisure Complex
Princess Margaret Way
Aberafan Seafront
Port Talbot
W. Glamorgan SA12 6QN
TEL: 0639 884141

Princess Royal Theatre
Civic Centre
Bethany Square
Port Talbot
W. Glamorgan SA13 1PJ
TEL: 0639 875200

PORTSMOUTH

Guildhall
Guildhall Square
Portsmouth PO1 2AB
TEL: 0705 834146

PRESTON

The Guild Hall
Lancaster Road
Preston PR1 1HT
TEL: 0772 203456

READING

The Hexagon
Queens Walk
Reading
Berks RG1 7UA
TEL: 0734 390123

REDHILL

Harlequin Theatre
Warwick Quadrant
Redhill
Surrey RH1 1NN
TEL: 0737 773721

SALISBURY

Salisbury City Hall
Malthouse Lane
Salisbury
Wilts SP2 7TU
TEL: 0722 334432

SCARBOROUGH

Open Air Theatre
Department of Tourism &
    Amenities
Londesborough Lodge
The Crescent
Scarborough YO11 2PW
TEL: 0723 369151

SCUNTHORPE

Scunthorpe Baths Hall
59 Doncaster Road
S. Humberside DN15 7RG
TEL: 0724 842332

SHEFFIELD

The Octagon Centre
Conference Office
The University of Sheffield
Sheffield S10 2TQ
TEL: 0742 824080

Sheffield City Hall
Barkers Pool
Sheffield S1 2JA
TEL: 0742 722885

SHEPTON MALLET

The Pavilion
Royal Bath & West
    Showground
Shepton Mallet
Somerset BA4 6QN
TEL: 0749 823211

SKEGNESS

Embassy Centre
Grant Parade
Skegness
Lincs PE25 2UG
TEL: 0754 768333

SOLIHULL

Solihull Conference Centre
Homer Road
Solihull
W. Midlands B91 3QN
TEL: 021–704 0088

SOUTHAMPTON

Southampton Guildhall
Civic Centre
Southampton
Hants SO9 4XF
TEL: 0703 832453

*University of Southampton
Conference Office*
Southampton
Hants SO9 5NH
TEL: 0703 595000

STIRLING

Stirling Management Centre
University of Stirling
Stirling FK9 4LA
TEL: 0786 451666

SOUTHPORT

*Southport Theatre & Floral
Hall Complex*
Promenade
Southport
Merseyside PR9 0DZ
TEL: 0704 540404

STOKE-ON-TRENT

Trentham Gardens
Stone Road
Trentham
Stoke-On-Trent
N. Staffs ST4 8AX
TEL: 0782 657341

ST ANDREWS

Crawford Arts Centre
93 North Street
St Andrews
Fife
Scotland KY16 9AL
TEL: 0334 74610

STOURBRIDGE

Hagley Hall
Hagley
Stourbridge
W. Midlands DY9 9LG
TEL: 0562 882408

ST AUSTELL

Cornwall Coliseum
Carlyon Bay
St Austell
Cornwall PL25 3RG
TEL: 0726 814261

SUNBURY-ON-THAMES

*Kempton Park Conference
Banqueting & Business Centre*
Sunbury-on-Thames
Middx TW16 5AE
TEL: 0932 786199

STEVENAGE

Gordon Craig Theatre
Stevenage Arts and Leisure
   Centre
Lytton Way
Stevenage
Herts SG1 1LZ
TEL: 0438 766642

SUNDERLAND

Empire Theatre
High Street West
Sunderland
Tyne & Wear SR1 3EX
TEL: 091–514 2517

SWANSEA

Brangwyn Hall
Guildhall Complex
Swansea
W. Glamorgan SA1 4PG
TEL: 0792 302489

SWINDON

Oasis Leisure Centre
North Star Avenue
Swindon
Wilts SN2 1EP
TEL: 0793 533406

TAUNTON

Brewhouse Theatre
Coal Orchard
Taunton
Somerset TA1 1JL
TEL: 0823 274608

TELFORD

Oakengates Theatre
Limes Walk
Oakengates
Telford
Shropshire TF2 6EP
TEL: 0952 610163

TEWKESBURY

Roses Theatre
Sun Street
Tewkesbury
Glos GL20 5NX
TEL: 0684 295074

TONBRIDGE

The Angel Centre
Angel Lane
Tonbridge
Kent TN9 SF1
TEL: 0732 359966

Penshurst Place Hotel
Penshurst Place
Tonbridge
Kent TN11 8DG
TEL: 0892 870307

TORQUAY

English Riviera Centre
Chestnut Avenue
Torquay
Devon TQ2 5LZ
TEL: 0803 299992

TWICKENHAM

Twickenham Banqueting &
Conference Centre
Rugby Road
Twickenham
Middx TW1 1DZ
TEL: 081–891 4565

UCKFIELD

The Bluebell Railway
Sheffield Park Station
Near Uckfield
E. Sussex TN22 3QL
TEL: 0825 723777

UXBRIDGE

Brunel University Conference Centre
Conference Office
Brunel University
Uxbridge
Middx UB8 3PH
TEL: 0895 274000 EXT. 2440

WARRINGTON

Parr Hall
Palmyra Square South
Warrington
Cheshire WA1 1BL
TEL: 0925 51178

WASHINGTON

Washington Leisure Centre
Town Centre
The Galleries
District 1
Washington
Tyne & Wear NE38 7SS
TEL: 091–4164318

WATFORD

Watford Assembly Halls
15 Hempstead Road
Watford
Herts WD1 3HA
TEL: 0923 226400

WELWYN

Brocket Hall
Welwyn
Herts AL8 7XG
TEL: 0707 335241

Fairway Tavern
Panshanger Golf Complex
Old Herns Lane
Welwyn Garden City
Herts AR7 2ED
TEL: 0707 333312

WIGAN

Wigan Pier
Wallgate
Wigan
Lancs WN3 4EU
TEL: 0942 323666

WINCHESTER

Theatre Royal
Jewry Street
Winchester
Hants SO23 8SB
TEL: 0962 842122

WINDSOR

Windsor Arts Centre
The Old Court
St Leonards Road
Windsor
Bucks SL4 3DB
TEL: 0753 859336

WOBURN

Woburn Abbey
Woburn
Beds MK43 0TP
TEL: 0525 290666

WOLVERHAMPTON

Civic & Wulfrun Halls
North Street
Wolverhampton WV1 1RQ
TEL: 0902 312029

Grand Theatre
Lichfield Street
Wolverhampton WV1 1DE
TEL: 0902 29212

YORK

Barbican Centre
Barbican Road
York YO1 4NT
TEL: 0904 628991

Conference Organisers and Producers

There are hundreds of companies to choose from, although most, as usual, are clustered around London inside the magic circle of the M25. The list given here includes at least a few of the regional companies – most of them as good and some of them better than their Big City colleagues. Two cautionary notes. The size of a production company does not necessarily indicate its ability to deliver the event you want; and in these recessionary times a list such as this must be regarded as a snapshot of a moment in time – the picture is constantly changing.

Bell Howe Conferences
1 Willoughby Street
Beeston
Nottingham NG9 2LT
TEL: 0602 436323

BPCE Conference & Exhibition Services
35 Broadwater Road
Twyford
Berks RG10 0EX
TEL: 0734 345704

CAL Communications Ltd
Conference House
9 Pavilion Parade
Brighton
W. Sussex BN2 1RA
TEL: 0273 623620

CEP Consultants Ltd
26 Albany Street
Edinburgh EH1 3QH
TEL: 031–557 2478

Commercial Presentations Group
Greater London House
Hampstead Road
London NW1 7QP
TEL: 071–383 5322

Communique Group
29 St Johns Lane
Smithfield
London EC1M 4BJ
TEL: 071–251 2229

Conference Associates & Services Ltd
Congress House
55 New Cavendish Street
London W1M 7RE
TEL: 071–486 0531

Conference Services North East
North East Farm Cottage
Great Whittington
Northumberland NE19 2HP
TEL: 0434 672307

Conference Live Ltd
6 Calico Row
Plantation Wharf
London SW11 3UF
TEL: 071–924 5550

Eureka Event Management
Barton House
East Cornworthy
Devon TQ9 7HF
TEL: 0804 22262

**The Event Organisation
Company**
8 Cotswold Mews
Battersea Square
London SW11 3RA
TEL: 071–228 8034

The Facilities Company
Suite 402
Butlers Wharf Business Centre
45 Curlew Street
London SE21 2ND
TEL: 071–357 6081

**Grosvenor Theatrical
Productions Ltd**
12 Sherwood Street
London W1V 7RD
TEL: 071–734 6755

Alistair S Haig
Marron House
Whaddon Hall
Whaddon
Bucks MK17 0NA
TEL: 0908 504779

HP: ICM
53 Frith Street
London W1V 5TE
TEL: 071–434 0929

Images Sight Sound Ltd
Parish Room Studios
Fairview Street
Cheltenham
Glos GL52 2JH
TEL: 0242 242133

Imagination Ltd
25 Store Street
South Crescent
London WC1E 7BL
TEL: 071–323 3300

JB Communications Group
15 Brackenbury Road
London W6 0BE
TEL: 081–749 6036

Joys Technical Services Ltd
De France Complex
St Saviours Road
St Saviours
Jersey
Channel Islands JE2 7LA
TEL: 0534 89072

**London Tourist Board &
Convention Bureau**
26 Grosvenor Gardens
Victoria
London SW1W 0DU
TEL: 071–730 3450

Mainstream Presentations
Eastgate
Castle Street
Castlefield
Manchester M3 4LZ
TEL: 061–832 7772

Mediatech
16 Northfield Industrial Estate
Beresford Avenue
Wembley
Middx HA0 1YH
TEL: 081–903 4372

**Meeting Point Conferences
Europe Ltd**
Third Floor
Eagle House
1–2 Parkshot
Richmond
Surrey TW9 2RD
TEL: 081–332 2600

Motivation
34A High Street
Thames Ditton
Surrey KT7 0UG
TEL: 081–398 7674

PCI Ltd
3–18 Harbour Yard
Chelsea Harbour
Chelsea
London SW10 0XD
TEL: 071–351 7755

Project Profile
Unit 103
Canalot Production Studios
222 Kensal Road
London W10 5BN
TEL: 081–969 7435

Purchasepoint
14–16 Peterborough Road
London SW6 3BN
TEL: 071–731 1377

**The Quad Production Co
(QPC)**
7 Bennell Court
West Street
Comberton
Cambs CB3 7DS
TEL: 0223 264445

RA Productions
3 Harlow View
Whinney Lane
Pannal Ash
Harrogate
North Yorkshire HG2 9LX
TEL: 0423 521593

Spectrum Communications Ltd
16–18 Acton Park Estate
Stanley Gardens
London W3 7QE
TEL: 081–740 4444

SSK – The Presentation Agency
111 Bell Street
Glasgow G4 0TD
TEL: 041–552 1177

Stanhope Associates
5 Alfred Road
Farnham
Surrey GU9 8ND
TEL: 0252 723562

Trident Exhibitions Ltd
West Devon Business Park
Brook Road
Tavistock
Devon PL19 9DP
TEL: 0822 614671

20/20 Productions
4 Harte Street Lane
Edinburgh EH1 3RN
TEL: 031–557 6996

Visual Connection (TVC) Ltd
1 Rostrevor Mews
London SW6 5AZ
TEL: 071–731 6300

Upstream Presentation Ltd
Ridings House
66 Alma Road
Windsor
Berks SL4 3EZ
TEL: 0753 858895

Miscellaneous Services

In this category you'll find just some of the suppliers who can provide a wide variety of products and services which the conference organiser will almost certainly need at some time or another. I've included here a few examples of the many reference books available to conference planners and organisers. At least one of these – preferably a collection – should be on every organiser's bookshelf.

Access All Areas
(The Events Trade Directory)
64–65 Great North Road
St Andrews
Bristol BS6 5AQ
TEL: 0272 428491

Aggreko Generators Ltd
Head Office
Overburn Avenue
Dumbarton
Strathclyde G82 2RL
TEL: 0389 67821

Alphabet Event Hire
(Mobile Exhibition &
Hospitality Units)
Station Road
North Kilworth
Nr Lutterworth
Leics LE17 6JA
TEL: 0280 703399

Association Meetings
International
Media House
The Square
Forest Row
Sussex RH18 5EP
TEL: 0342 824044

Autocue Ltd
Autocue House
265 Merton Road
London SW18 5JS
TEL: 081–870 0104

Bannerama – the Backdrop
Hire Company
4a Mitre Avenue
Rear of 2 Greenleaf Road
London E17 6QG
TEL: 081–520 7209

Benns Media Directory
Benn House
Sovereign Way
Tonbridge
Kent TN9 1RW
TEL: 0732 362666

Conference and Incentive Travel
22 Lancaster Gate
London W2 3LP
TEL: 071–413 4307

Conference Blue Book/
Green Book
Riverbank House
Angel Lane
Tonbridge
Kent TN9 1SE
TEL: 0732 362666

EDS Portaprompt Ltd
Lane End Road
Sands
High Wycombe
Bucks HP12 4JQ
TEL: 0494 450414

Exhibition Graphics
(Signs and Graphics)
30 Grove Place
London W3 6AS
TEL: 081–992 9842

Expo World International Ltd
(Modular and portable display
systems)
Standard House
107/115 Eastmoor Street
London SE7 8LX
TEL: 081–293 3411

Holographics Ltd
(Holograms and Holography)
32 Lexington Street
Soho
London W1R 3HR
TEL: 071–437 8992

Howorth Wrightson Ltd
'Props'
Unit 2
Cricket Street
Denton
Manchester M34 3DR
TEL: 061–335 0220

IQ Professional Prompting
2 Beeston Street
Castle Northwich
Cheshire
CW8 1HB
TEL: 0606 871444

QTV Prompting Ltd
The Barn
Handpost Farmhouse
Maidens Green
Nr Bracknell
Berks RG12 6LD
TEL: 0344 890470

Studio and TV Hire
(Period and modern props)
3 Ariel Way
Wood Lane
London W12 7SL
TEL: 081–749 3445

The White Book
PO Box 55
Staines
Middlesex TW18 4UG
TEL: 0784 464441

Venue Directory
PO BOX 553
Rainham
Kent ME8 9AR
TEL: 0634 235671

Trade Organisations

The great Dr Johnson said there are two kinds of knowledge; we either know a subject ourselves, or we know where we can find information upon it. Conference organisers with insufficient knowledge of the bewildering variety of specialist products or facilities available should make contact with an appropriate Trade Organisation which should be able to provide all the necessary information.

Arts Council of Great Britain
14 Great Peter Street
London SW1P 3NQ
TEL: 071–333 0100

Arts Council of Northern Ireland
185 Stranmill Road
Belfast BT9 5DU
TEL: 0232 381591

Association of British Professional Conference Organisers (ABPCO)
54 Church Street
Tisbury
Wilts SP3 6NH
TEL: 0747 870490

Association of British Theatre Technicians (ABTT)
47 Bermondsey Street
London SE1 3XT
TEL: 071–403 3778

Association of Conference Executives (ACE)
Riverside House
High Street
Huntingdon
Cambs PE18 6SG
TEL: 0480 457595

Association of Exhibition Organisers
26 Chapter Street
London SW1P 4ND
TEL: 071–932 0252

Association of Lighting Designers
3 Apollo Studios
Charlton Kings Road
London NW5 2SW
TEL: 071–482 4224

Audio Visual Association (AVA)
Fox Talbot House
2 Amwell End
Ware
Herts SG12 9HN
TEL: 0920 468832

British Association of Conference Towns
First Floor
Elizabeth House
22 Suffolk Street
Queensway
Birmingham B15 1LS
TEL: 021–616 1400

British Department of Trade and Industry
Ashdown House
123 Victoria Street
London SW1E 6RB
TEL: 071–215 5000

British Exhibition Contractors Association (BECA)
Kingsmere House
Graham Road
Wimbledon
London SW19 3SR
TEL: 081–543 3888

British Interactive Multimedia Association
6 Washingley Road
Folksworth
Peterborough PE7 3SY
TEL: 0733 245700

Confederation of British Industry (CBI)
Centre Point
103 New Oxford Street
London WC1A 1DU
TEL: 071–379 7400

Corporate Hospitality Association Ltd
PO Box 76
Kingswood
Tadworth
Surrey KT20 6LF
TEL: 0737 833963

The Designers and Art Directors Association
Graphic Square
85 Vauxhall Road
London SE11 5HJ
TEL: 071–582 6487

The Directors Guild of Great Britain
Suffolk House
1–8 Whitfield Place
London W1P 5SF
TEL: 071–383 3858

English Tourist Board
Thames Tower
Blacks Road
Hammersmith
London W6 9EL
TEL: 081–846 9000

Event Suppliers Association (TESA)
29 Market Place
Wantage
Oxon OX12 8BG
TEL: 0235 772207

International Visual Communications Association (IVCA)
Bolsover House
5–6 Clipstone Street
London W1P 7EB
TEL: 071–580 0962

Mechanical Copyright Protection Society (MCPS)
Elgar House
41 Streatham High Road
Streatham
London SW16 1ER
TEL: 081–769 4400

Mobile & Outside Caterer's Association
180 Lincoln Road North
Olton
Folihull
Birmingham B27 6RP
TEL: 021–693 7000

National Exhibitors Association
29A Market Square
Biggleswade
Beds SG18 8AQ
TEL: 0767 316255

**National Outdoor Events
Association**
7 Hamilton Way
Wallington
Surrey SM6 9NY
TEL: 081–669 8121

**Performing Rights Society
(PRS)**
29–33 Berners Street
London W1P 4AA
TEL: 071–580 5544

Phonographic Performance Ltd
Ganton House
14–22 Ganton Street
London W1V 1LB
TEL: 071–437 0311

**Professional Lighting & Sound
Association**
7 Highlight House
St Leonards Road
Eastbourne
E. Sussex BN21 3UH
TEL: 0323 410335

**Society of Incentive Travel
Executives**
42 Clifden Road
Twickenham
Middx TW1 4LX
TEL: 081–744 2312

**Sound & Communications
Industries Federation**
4-B High Street
Burnham
Slough
Berks SL1 7JH
TEL: 0628 667633

St John Ambulance
1 Grosvenor Crescent
London SW1X 7EF
TEL: 071–235 5321

Writers' Guild of Great Britain
430 Edgware Road
London W2 1EH
TEL: 071–723 8074

Sound Services

Whatever kind of audience you're addressing, good sound is vitally important if you're aiming to put your message across effectively. Don't be dazzled by fearsome banks of technical equipment when choosing a sound specialist to work with; it's far more important that the engineer is sympathetic to your needs and can speak your language; equipment is important, but skill is vital.

Audio Visual Communications (Gatwick)
Unit 1, Alpine Works
Oak Road
Southgate
Crawley
W. Sussex RH11 8AJ
TEL: 0293 525123

Audio Visual Communications Limited
412 Montrose Avenue Trading Estate
Slough
Berks SL1 4TJ
TEL: 0753 821351

AVE Business Presentations
16 Southsea Road
Kingston
Surrey KT1 2EH
TEL: 081–549 7521

Cloud One PA Services Limited
19 Jameson Road
Aston
Birmingham B6 7SJ
TEL: 021–326 6456

Concert Sound Limited
Unit 4
Shakespeare Industrial Estate
Shakespeare Street
Watford
Herts WD2 5HD
TEL: 0923 240854

Delta Conference Systems
Unit 4, Springside
Rue de la Monnait
Trinity
Jersey JE3 5OG
Channel Islands
TEL: 0534 865885

Drinkle & Mann Sound Engineering
Hire Department
Unit 2
Peel Green Trading Estate
Eccles
Manchester M30 7HF
TEL: 061–707 7588

Entec Sound & Light
517 Yeading Lane
Northolt
Middx UB5 6LN
TEL: 081–842 4004

MAC Sound
1–2 Attenbury's Park
Park Road
Altrincham
Cheshire WA14 5QE
TEL: 061–969 8311

Mike Weaver Communications Ltd
17 Redland Close
Aldermans Green Industrial
  Estate
Coventry CV2 2NP
TEL: 0203 602605

Powerhouse
247 Oakleigh Road North
Whetstone
London N20 0TX
TEL: 081–368 9852

Pro-Audio Systems
Unit M7
Enterprise 5 Industrial Park
Five Lane Ends
Idle
Bradford BD10 8BW
TEL: 0274 621242

RMPA (Worcester)
42 Lower Ferry Lane
Callow End
Worcs WR2 4UN
TEL: 0905 831877

SAV Limited
Party House
Mowbray Drive
Blackpool FY3 7JR
TEL: 0253 302602

Sound Hire (Scotland)
Hill Barnes
Dunfield Road
Blairgowrie PH10 6SA
TEL: 0250 873988

Sound Marketing
18 Capitol House
Heigham Street
Norwich NR2 4TE
TEL: 0603 667725

Sound Plus
193 Straight Road
Romford
Essex RM3 7JJ
TEL: 0708 372013

System Sound
8 The Arches
Kew Bridge
Richmond
Surrey TW9 3AW
TEL: 081–940 5348

Willpower PA Systems Limited
Unit 4 Acorn Productions
  Centre
105 Blundell Street
London N7 9BN
TEL: 071–609 9870

Wise Productions
13–15 Pensbury Street
London SW8 4TL
TEL: 081–978 1223

722027 (Lighting & Sound Equipment)
118 Cowley Road
Oxford OX4 1JE
TEL: 0865 722027

Lighting

Do you simply want to hire lights and you know what you want? Or do you need someone who can provide the skill and facilities to light an event you are organising? The names listed here should be able to help you do either. If you are planning to call in a specialist to handle all your lighting requirements, do it as early as you can; it could save you money.

Audio Visual Communications Limited
412 Montrose Avenue Trading Estate
Slough
Berks SL1 4TJ
TEL: 0753 821351

The AV Company
278 Forest Road
Walthamstow
London E17 5JN
TEL: 081–520 4321

AVE Business Presentations
16 Southsea Road
Kingston
Surrey KT1 2EH
TEL: 081–549 7521

Centre Stage
18 Burlington Road
Chiswick
London W4 4BG
TEL: 081–747 8678

Gear Hire Sound & Light
Unit 3, Cooke Close
South Lowestoft Industrial Estate
Pakefield
Lowestoft
Suffolk NR33 7NA
TEL: 0502 585375

Gearhouse Limited
17 Penn Street
Birmingham B4 7RJ
TEL: 021–333 3390

JBE Stage Lighting & Equipment Company
7 Rose Way
Purdeys
Rochford
Essex SS4 1LY
TEL: 0702 545826

Kave Lighting
Unit 10
Sheddingdean Business Centre
Marchants Way
Burgess Hill
W. Sussex RH15 8QY
TEL: 0444 871180

Kent & Sussex Sound & Lighting
8 Tollgate Buildings
Hadlow Road
Tonbridge
Kent TN9 1NX
TEL: 0732 360234

Limelight Services Limited
Unit 6
Manfield Park Industrial Estate
Guildford Road
Cranleigh
Surrey GU6 8PA
TEL: 0483 275612

Alan McGregor
15 Padmoor Court
Sydenham
Leamington Spa CV31 1QP
TEL: 0926 450994

**MSS PA & Lighting Services
Limited
(McLeod Sound Services)**
44 Queens Road
Hertford
Herts SG13 8AZ
TEL: 0992 583806

Northern Lighting Systems
Unit 7
Woodend Avenue Industrial
    Estate
Woodend Avenue
Speke
Liverpool L24 9NB
TEL: 051–448 1523

Pearce Hire
Unit 27, Second Dove
    Industrial Estate
Ferngate
Peterborough
Cambs PE1 5XA
TEL: 0733 54950

Playlight Hire Limited
19 Gorst Road
Park Royal
London NW10 6LA
TEL: 081–965 8188

Roadshow Promotions
7 Market Walk
Saffron Walden
Essex CB10 1JZ
TEL: 0799 526343

Seeing is Believing
3 Alexander House
CCE Complex
Windmill Lane
Denton
Manchester M34 3QS
TEL: 061–335 9131

Syrett Neon International
Unit H4
Springhead Industrial Park
Springhead Road
Northfleet
Kent DA11 8HL
TEL: 0474 334781

White Light Northern
Corporation Street
Sowerby Bridge
W. Yorks HX6 2QQ
TEL: 0422 839651

Computer Graphics

This is one of the fastest-growing sectors in the corporate communications field and it would be impossible to attempt a comprehensive list of specialist companies. Most, but certainly not all, are in or around London, and many are equally skilled at creating and/or manipulating images for video and 35mm slides.

Applied Visual Technologies Ltd
Pyramid House
1 Martindale Road
Hounslow West
Middlesex TW7 6ER
TEL: 081–575 5900

Audionics
The Studio
Lonacre
Headley Road
Grayshott
Surrey GU26 6JG
TEL: 0428 713937

Design Group
Mill House
Haddricks Mill Road
South Gosforth
Newcastle-upon-Tyne
NE3 1QL
TEL: 091–284 5334

Harris Media
9 Denton Road
Canton
Cardiff CF5 1PD
TEL: 0222 341830

JB Communications Group
15 Brackenbury Road
London W6 0BE
TEL: 081–749 6036

Magic Lantern Group
Metropolitan Wharf (BG)
Wapping Wall
London E1 9SS
TEL: 071–480 6811

The Moving Picture Company
25 Noel Street
London W1V 3RD
TEL: 071–434 3100

The Original Graphic Company
8 Golden Square
London W1R 3AF
TEL: 071–839 5003

Rushes
66 Old Compton Street
London W1V 5PA
TEL: 071–437 8676

Sarner International
32 Woodstock Grove
Shepherds Bush
London W12 8LE
TEL: 081–743 1288

Television Services International (TSI)
10 Grape Street
London WC2H 8DY
TEL: 071–379 3445

Theatre and Stage Effects Suppliers

When you're planning something special, these are just some of the experts you might consult – their valuable knowledge and experience is yours for the asking. Don't forget that some special effects need special precautions. The specialists listed here will tell you what's required and may even offer to provide expert help and guidance on the spot for a nominal fee.

Absolute Action Limited
Mantle House
Broomhill Road
Wandsworth
London SW18 4JQ
TEL: 081–871 5005

Astra Fireworks
Unit 5
2 Sandwich Industrial Estate
Sandwich
Kent CT13 9LY
TEL: 0304 614130

Blackwood's Party Planning
PO Box 87
Henley-on-Thames
Oxon RG9 6JQ
TEL: 0491 638412

British Turntable Company Limited
Emblem Works
Emblem Street
Bolton
Lancs BL3 5BW
TEL: 0204 25626

Cryoservice Limited
Blackpole Trading Estate East
Blackpole Road
Worcs WR3 8SG
TEL: 0905 754500

Environetics Unlimited
68 Brookfield Road
Hucclecote
Glos GL3 3HQ
TEL: 0452 611074

Fantastic Fireworks
Rocket House
Redbourn
St Albans
Herts AL3 7RH
FAX: 0582 485545

Ice Cooling (Dry Ice) Limited
Unicool House
143 Guildford Road
West End
Woking
Surrey GU24 9LS
TEL: 0483 797658

JBE Stage Lighting & Equipment Company
7 Rose Way
Purdeys
Rochford
Essex SS4 1LY
TEL: 0702 545826

Laser Magic
2 Church Street
LM House
Seaford
E. Sussex BN25 1HD
TEL: 0323 890752

MG Gas Products Limited
Cedar House
39 London Road
Reigate
Surrey RH2 9QE
TEL: 0737 241133

Midland Theatre Services
Junction 1 Industrial Estate
Darmouth Road
Smethwick
Birmingham B66 1AX
TEL: 021–525 4545

Northern Light
79 Loan-Bank Quadrant
Govan
Glasgow G51 3HZ
TEL: 041–440 1771

Pains Fireworks Ltd
The Old Chapel
Romsey Road
Whiteparish
Wilts SP5 2SD
TEL: 091–261 1545

Theme Makers Ltd
The Folly
Pinner Hill Road
Pinner
Middx HA5 3YQ
TEL: 081–429 3000

Audio Visual Production

Once again, this list is just a small selection from the vast number of companies operating in this field. Most are in the equipment hire business too, so they'll not only take your brief and turn it into an effective AV presentation, they'll also hire you the necessary equipment for an AV show – screens, projectors, remote control units etc – and professional crews to set up the equipment and operate it on the day.

Audio Visual Communications (Gatwick) Limited
Unit 1, Alpine Works
Oak Road
Southgate
Crawley
W. Sussex RH11 8AJ
TEL: 0293 525123

Autocue Limited
Autocue House
265 Merton Road
London SW18 5JS
TEL: 081–870 0104

AVE Business Presentations
16 Southsea Road
Kingston
Surrey KT1 2EH
TEL: 081–549 7521

Bodley Knose Limited
Unit 2
The Pines Trading Estate
Broad Street
Guildford
Surrey GU3 3BH
TEL: 0483 504868

Business Vision Ltd
Astech House
The Forge
Binsted
Hants GU34 4PS
TEL: 0420 22500

Clicks
10 Bakers Yard
Bakers Row
London EC1R 3DD
TEL: 071–278 2300

Commercial Presentations Group
Greater London House
Hampstead Road
London NW1 7QP
TEL: 071–383 5322

Drake Group of Companies
Audio Visual Department
St Fagans Road
Fairwater
Cardiff CF5 3AE
TEL: 0222 560333

Edric Audio Visual
34–36 Oak End Way
Gerrards Cross
Bucks SL9 8BR
TEL: 0753 884646

Fisher Audio Visual
267–269 Old Chester Road
Birkenhead
Merseyside L42 3TD
TEL: 051–644 8585

Gateway Audio Visual
472 Green Lanes
London N13 5XF
TEL: 081–882 0177

Hanimex (UK) Limited
Audio Visual Division
Hanimex House
Faraday Road
Dorcan
Swindon
Wilts SN3 5HW
TEL: 0793 526211

Imagination Limited
25 Store Street
South Crescent
London WC1E 7BL
TEL: 071–323 3300

Joys Production Services
Le Foulon Road
St Peter Port
Guernsey
Channel Islands GY1 1YR
TEL: 0481 727117

McMillan UK Limited
Unit 11
Telford Court
9 South Avenue
Clydbank Business Park
Glasgow G81 2NR
TEL: 041–952 2222

Nile Productions
Five Towns Resource &
  Technology Centre
Wellbeek Street
Castleford
W. Yorks WF10 1DR
TEL: 0977 519625

Project Profile
Unit 103
Canalot Production Studios
222 Kensal Road
London W10 5BN
TEL: 081–969 7435

Rapier Productions
17–21 Emerald Street
London WC1N 3QL
TEL: 071–405 6979

Sarner Audio Visual
32 Woodstock Grove
Shepherds Bush
London W12 8LE
TEL: 081–743 1288

Saville Group Limited
Unit 3
Castleton Close
Armley Road
Leeds
Yorks LS12 2DS
TEL: 0532 461712

SSK Ltd
111 Bell Street
Glasgow G4 0TD
TEL: 041–552 1177

Spoken Image Ltd
The Design Centre
44 Canal Street
Manchester M1 3WD
TEL: 061–236 7522

**Theatre Projects Services
Limited**
20–22 Fairway Drive
Greenford
Middx UB6 8PW
TEL: 081–575 5555

**Visual Connection (TVC)
Limited**
1 Rostrevor Mews
London SW6 5AZ
TEL: 071–731 6300

Xpressions
8 Guildersfield Road
London SW16 5LT
TEL: 081–764 1779

20/20 Productions
4 Hart Street Lane
Edinburgh EH1 3RN
TEL: 031–557 6996

Translation Services

When you've selected a translation service, here are three tips to help you get the best out of it: try to avoid rush jobs; it's how mistakes happen and it increases the price. If there's an unusual language or a great deal of technical language involved, allow more time. Complex technical language may cost more too. And please provide clean, typed copy if at all possible!

Amherst Conference Services
33 Amherst Road
London W13 8LX
TEL: 081–998 3103

Apple Sound
Unit 3
Cambrian Business Park
Queens Lane
Bromfield Industrial Estate
Mold
Clwyd CH7 1NJ.
TEL: 0352 700433

Brahler ICS (UK) Limited
Unit 12, Ronald Rolph Court
Wadlows Road
Cambridge CB5 8PX
TEL: 0223 411601

Charrondiere Translations
20 Pownall Gardens
Hounslow
Middx TW3 1YW
TEL: 081–577 6438

Conference Interpreters Group
10 Barley Mow Passage
London W4 4PH
TEL: 081–995 0801

Dragonfly Communications
13 Barclay Square
London W1X 5HG
TEL: 071–629 8471

German Accurate Translations
81 Chambers Lane
London NW10 2RN
TEL: 081–459 5023

Indo Lingua Services Limited
112 Leighton Road
Kentish Town
London NW5 2RG
TEL: 071–267 8152

Interspanish
8 St Martin's Close
Alms Houses
Bayham Street
London NW1 0BD
TEL: 071–485 3804

Linguistlink Limited
Linburn House
71 Hawstead Road
London SE6 4JL
TEL: 071–328 9426

M & R Conference Communications
7 Bell Industrial Estate
50 Cunnington Street
London W4 5HB
TEL: 081–995 4714

Sally Walker Language Services
43 St Nicholas Street
Bristol BS1 1TP
TEL: 0272 291594

Transtelex
Marzell House
116–128 North End Road
London W14 9PP
TEL: 071–381 0967

Unique Freelance Secretaries
766 Finchley Road
London NW11 7TH
TEL: 081–455 8187

Westminster Sound
17 Canterbury Grove
London SE27 0NT
TEL: 0753 553325

Video Production Companies

By all means be impressed by the contents of the showreel, but don't take it for granted that the people who made those programmes will work on yours. Ask lots of questions and get to know the people who'll be doing *your* work. Give a good, clear brief (see pages 52–55) – and try to avoid asking 'How Much?' before the producer has had a chance to read it!

ANV Productions
47A Kendal Street
London W2 2BU
TEL: 071–262 3074

CAL Communications Limited
Conference House
Pavilion Parade
Brighton
E. Sussex BN2 1RF
TEL: 0273 747888

Chatsworth TV Limited
97–99 Dean Street
London W1V 5RA
TEL: 071–734 4302

Cheerleader Productions
Room 356
Northcliffe House
2 Derry Street
London W8 5TT
TEL: 081–995 7778

Commercial Presentations Group
Greater London House
Hampstead Road
London NW1 7QP
TEL: 071–383 5322

Complete Communications
Communications House
Garsington Road
Cowley
Oxford OX4 2NG
TEL: 0865 778966

Crown Productions
Barn Studios
East Bergholt
Colchester
Essex CO7 6XU
TEL: 0206 298979

CTVC
Hillside
Merry Hill Road
Bushey
Watford WD2 1DR
TEL: 081–950 4426

Diverse Productions
6 Gorleston Street
London W14 8XS
TEL: 071–603 4567

Edinburgh Film and Video Productions
Ninbe Mile Burn
By Penicuik
Midlothian EH26 9LT
TEL: 0968 672131

216

Fiti-Tifi
37–39 Bangor Street
Caernarvon
Gwynedd LL5 1AR
TEL: 0286 677469

Greystoke Productions
195 Euston Road
London NW1 2BN
TEL: 071–388 8561

Hammerhead
9 Merchaiston Mews
Edinburgh EH10 4PE
TEL: 031–229 5000

Head to Head Communication Ltd
The Hook
Five Ways Business Centre
Plane Tree Crescent
Feltham
Middx TW13 7AQ
TEL: 081–893 7766

Insight Productions Ltd
Gidleigh Studio
Gidleigh
Chagford
Newton Abbot
Devon TQ13 8HP
TEL: 0647 432686

JB Communications Group
15 Brackenbury Road
London W6 0BE
TEL: 081–749 6036

Landseer Film & TV Productions Ltd
140 Royal College Street
London NW1 0TA
TEL: 071–485 7333

Meditel Productions Ltd
Bedford Chambers
The Piazza
Covent Garden
London WC2E 8HA
TEL: 071–836 9216

Michael Barratt Ltd
Profile House
5–7 Forlease Road
Maidenhead
Berks SL6 1RP
TEL: 0628 770800

The Moving Picture Company
25 Noel Street
London W1V 3RD
TEL: 071–434 3100

North West Video Productions
9A New Street
Carnforth
Lancs LA5 9BX
TEL: 0524 735774

Picture Palace Productions Ltd
53 Brewer Street
London W1R 3FD
TEL: 071–439 9882

Presentation Communications International Ltd
3–18 Harbour Yard
Chelsea Harbour
London SW10 0XD
TEL: 071–351 7755

Rapier Productions
17–21 Emerald Street
London WC1N 3QL
TEL: 071–405 6979

Rob Harris Productions
Unit 7, Walmer Studios
235 Walmer Road
London W11 4EY
TEL: 071–792 3381

SSK Ltd
111 Bell Street
Glasgow G4 0TQ
TEL: 041–552 1177

The Visual Connection (TVC) Ltd
1 Rostrevor Mews
London SW6 5AZ
TEL: 071–731 6300

Wadlow Grosvenor International Ltd
18 Grosvenor Street
London W1X 9FD
TEL: 071–409 1225

Watermark
Mann Island House
Mann Island
Pier Head
Liverpool L3 1DG
TEL: 051–236 7757

Wyatt Cattaneo Productions
22 Charing Cross Road
London WC2H 0HR
TEL: 071–379 6444

YPL Communications Ltd
Tong Hall
Tong
Nr Bradford
W. Yorks BD4 0RR
TEL: 0532 854394

Set Design and Construction

These are just some of the companies that can help you transform an ordinary venue into an exciting environment. If possible, involve them at an early stage; the set designer may have ideas that could make life easier for the writer, the producer and the participants – ideas that might even save time and money too.

AVE Business Presentations Ltd
16 Southsea Road
Kingston
Surrey KT1 2EH
TEL: 081–549 7521

Bailey Redman Scenery
15 Barratt Street
Easton
Bristol BS5 6DE
TEL: 0272 513679

Bob Jessamine
4 Matlock Avenue
Southport
Merseyside PR8 5EZ
TEL: 0704 564521

Kew Workshop Company Limited
Station Yard
Kew Gardens
Surrey TW9 3QB
TEL: 081–948 3367

Project Profile
Unit 103
Canalot Production Studios
222 Kensal Road
London W10 5BN
TEL: 081–969 7435

Sound & Vision AV Limited
11B South Gyle Crescent
South Gyle Industrial Estate
Edinburgh EH12 9EB
TEL: 031–334 3324

SSK Ltd
111 Bell Street
Glasgow G4 0TQ
TEL: 041–552 1177

Staging and Event
Unit 27
Poplar Drive
Witton
Birmingham B6 7AD
TEL: 021–344 3473

Upstage
Unit 6
27a Spring Grove Road
Hounslow
Middx TW3 4BE
TEL: 081–572 1919

INDEX

About the Author:

Robin O'Connor has worked as a freelance writer/director since 1975. He has written several broadcast TV programmes as well as a great deal of material for the corporate market. He has written and directed many conference events, ranging from seminars and business presentations to spectacular product launches, large-scale AGMs and awards ceremonies both here and abroad. His credits also include award-winning video and audio visual programmes, a variety of corporate communication publications, and training and information programmes for many leading UK companies. He is currently writing and producing a number of communications packages for the Home Office Central Planning and Training Unit.